STUCK
ON THE
STOCK MARKET
THE BEGINNERS GUIDE TO
UNDERSTANDING THE STOCK MARKET

SECRETS ON HOW TO START INVESTING IN THE STOCK MARKET

By

Edward R. Williams

To my dad, Edward R. Williams Sr, a loving man of God and one of the world's greatest entrepreneurs. This book would not exist without your teaching and mentoring.

It is a tribute to who you are.

And also to my queen, Ekaterina, my sons, Cristiano, Sterling, Winston, and my daughters Angelina and Edison: I am so proud, and I love each of you with all of my heart.

Praise for *Stuck on the Stock Market*

"*Stuck on the Stock Market* is a must-read for leaders and business owners who desire their personal finances to be thriving along with their high-performing businesses. The concepts in this book have allowed me to not only maintain my focus on making my business the best it can be, but also to be the best family man I can be at the same time. *Stuck on the Stock Market* is like no other finance book because it offers real, practical, easy-to-understand concepts of how to build wealth. These tools have been an invaluable resource for my family. This book will change your life." **- Christopher "CJ" Gross**, *instructor at St. Bonaventure University, Harvard Business Review writer, TEDx Speaker, and founder and CEO of Ascension Worldwide.*

CONTENTS

INTRODUCTION

Growing up as a black kid in the inner city of Baltimore, Maryland, in the early '80s, the stock market was a foreign concept to me as flying in an airplane. I knew planes could go up and down but everything in between how it worked was a mystery. I remember flying on an airplane for the first time with my parents to Hawaii. My dad was a taxicab driver, and my mom was a secretary, so having enough money to fly was a big deal! When boarding the airplane, I was incredibly nervous because I didn't understand how an aircraft could stay in the sky for hours carrying the weight of passengers and luggage. I had a million questions in my head. What if we ran out of gas? What if the engine stopped running? What if the wind blew too hard? The only thing that gave me a little confidence was the crowd of people at the airports. Everyone seemed relaxed and carefree, so they must know something I didn't. I knew the only route to paradise, Hawaii, must be traveled in a plane, and I was willing to take the risk because others did, and I wanted the same results they received of fun in the sun.

The stock market can pull many of the same feelings out from individuals of fears and nervousness, from going along with the crowd to contemplating risk versus reward. I was different. I didn't have any of these considerations because I never participated in investing, so it didn't exist in my world. The stock market seemed so complicated from afar, and generally, when something is too complicated, it's human nature to "do nothing" and not participate. Growing up in my household, we never discussed participating in the stock market. I didn't know anyone who invested. The only reason I knew it existed was from watching movies about people making lots of money investing, and I wanted to have the same money, power, and respect they gained from the stock market.

Being in an environment solely focused on surviving, I didn't see the value of investing. Why should I care about the stock market? Investing appeared to be a luxury that was not necessary for my circumstances. Why would anyone care about the stock market when you can do fine without it? This is what I told myself throughout my college years up until I had kids. The problem with that philosophy is "I didn't know what I didn't know!" Now I understand through the stock market that the interest from a pile of money can potentially earn me more money than a steady paycheck if I'm willing to take a calculated risk. It signifies ownership and potential for increased earnings.

The purpose of the stock market is to provide investors the opportunity to share in the profits of publicly traded companies. Another important purpose of the stock market is to provide capital to companies that can fund and expand their businesses. In other words, the stock market is valuable to anyone who wants to share the profits of other businesses without getting involved in all of the day-to-day operations, or for business owners who want extra money to help their companies grow. I can hear your thoughts. What's the catch? What if the companies I invest in decline in value? How can I afford to invest in the stock market?

There are risks to everything in life, including investing in the stock market. There was a risk with me flying on the airplane as a kid, but I ended up in Hawaii swimming with dolphins, drinking out of coconuts, and experiencing the world's most beautiful waterfalls. I'm not equating stock market risk with the risk of flying because they both have a completely different set of risks. The takeaway is to always measure the relationship between risks and rewards.

I saw my dad work his entire life until the day before his death at age 76. If he had learned about the stock market, he would have had an opportunity to compound his income, provide more economic freedom, and live a much more comfortable life.

This book is designed to explain the stock market so someone with no experience and little means of investing can be exposed to how it all works and not feel intimidated, and instead, opening their lives to a world of financial possibilities. I will not tell you the stock market is safe, and you have nothing to worry about. People often told me statistics proving flying is much safer than riding in a car so I should feel assured, but that did not make me less nervous to fly because I do not want to be safe 9 times out of 10 or 99 percent of the time. What happens if my fight is the 1 percent?

However, once I learned in detail the forces of flight such as lift, thrust, drag, and weight, I realized turbulence is nothing more than variations of wind and an aircraft is designed to endure forces far greater than any weather system one can expect to encounter. Knowledge is empowering and I'm now able to stomach flying, allowing me to enjoy the world's finest destinations. I'm still nervous on a plane but less nervous since I understand how it works.

My mission is to provide an easy-to-understand household book that can get families closer to financial freedom through a full understanding of the stock market. This book will dispel the myths and limiting beliefs that have kept this practical information off dinner tables.

You will learn:

• The history of the stock market

• How stocks are traded

• How to open accounts

• How to read financial statements and market indexes

• How to analyze stocks and the risk associated

• How to profit from the market, where to start, and tips for beginners

Most individuals are interested in profits, therefore profiting from the stock market will be discussed in detail, but this isn't a "get rich quick" book. Investors can only profit from stock buying in one of two ways, and it generally takes time to build sustainable wealth. Some stocks pay regular dividends, which means the company has a profit and they pay some of that profit to the shareholders in the form of regular payments. The other way investors can profit from buying stocks is by selling their stock at a higher price than they paid.

Let's begin.

CHAPTER 1

Misconceptions about the Stock Market

T he stock market has continued to be an investment vehicle favored by banks, large corporations, and some of the world's wealthiest individuals. What do they know that you don't know? We've all heard something about the stock market. Everyone has an opinion. The problem is that when we learn something new, we use our prior knowledge to help make sense of the new information. What if our prior knowledge about the stock market came from non-credible sources? When our prior knowledge is inaccurate, we're more likely to misinterpret, misunderstand or disregard new information.

Since you're reading this book, you're already several steps ahead, so let's remove any barriers preventing you from learning life-changing information. Misconceptions about the stock market can greatly influence how new information is interpreted. For years I've been discussing common misconceptions about the stock market that can be detrimental to one's financial success. I am here to dispel the misconceptions so you can have greater chances of your money working for you.

The top five misconceptions about the stock market I've heard over the years are:

1. Investing in the stock market is like gambling

2. You can time the market

3. Investing is too complicated and time-consuming

4. Investing is for the rich

5. It's safer to keep money in a savings account

Do you believe any of these common misconceptions? Let's unpack each myth.

Investing in the stock market is like gambling. It might look similar because both involve taking risks for a chance to earn more than you put in. However, there are major differences. Over a long time horizon, time is in favor of the investor, whereas gambling is the opposite. A long time horizon is generally in favor of the lottery or casino. Other differences are that there are things you can do to help manage the amount of risk when investing. Some types of risk can be managed with diversification, which is spreading your money out among different stocks and investments, such as bonds and short-term investments.

In a 2013 letter to shareholders, Warren Buffet wrote: "The goal of the nonprofessional should not be to pick winners—neither he nor his "helpers" can do that—but should rather be to own a cross-section of businesses that in the aggregate are bound to do well." Don't worry if you don't know the differences yet among stocks, bonds, and short-term investments because I will elaborate more in the next chapter. The bottom line is these things can reduce the amount of risk in your mix. With gambling, you don't have much control. You can only reduce the wager, but you cannot reduce the risk. The moral difference between the two is that investing increases the overall wealth of an economy, and gambling takes money from a loser and gives it to a winner.

You can time the market. I'm sure many of you have heard this before, "I will wait for the best time to get in the stock market." Despite what social media might tell you, no one knows what the market is going to do. If someone knew when the market would go up and down, they would be the most powerful person on the planet. Most people can't even predict how their spouses will react to certain news. Can you imagine trying to predict how millions of investors will react and predict the exact time of their reaction? Instead of trying to pick the perfect time to buy and sell, generally, the best route for long-term success is to plan and stay the course. The stock market, over time, has increased in value. Waiting for the best time can lead to many missed opportunities. as missing just two of the best days in the market can significantly impact your long-term returns.

Investing is too complicated and time-consuming. This is the easiest statement to disprove. To correct this misconception a better statement would be: "Investment advising can be complicated and time-consuming." Researching companies and reviewing risks, such as financial, reputation, regulatory, before you decide to purchase shares can be complicated and time-consuming. The good news is there are investment advisors who spend 70-hour weeks analyzing companies, and they build a mix for you to invest in. All you must do is meet with them once a year for a review. Investing can be quick and easy.

Investing is for the rich. This is a psychological and emotional pitfall that can be solved with education. It has never been cheaper for anyone to invest, even if money is tight. **Thanks to the emergence of zero-commission online brokers and robo-advisors, anyone can invest with just a small amount of money. Robo-advisors are generally online services that provide automated portfolios based on your investment preferences.** Investment minimums are nonexistent for many mutual funds, and exchange-traded funds (ETFs) offer another way to invest with no minimum fees. We will discuss mutual funds and ETFs in chapter 5. At many financial institutions, it's possible to start investing with just a few dollars— even with professional investment management.

It's safer to keep money in a savings account. Cash is not as safe as most people think. Putting too much money in a savings account means your ability to purchase items decreases with inflation. Inflation is the rate of increase in prices over a given period of time. For example, if the bulk of your money is in a savings account earning 1% and inflation is over 7%, you're losing 6% of your money. The stock market can be a wise place to put extra money after you have an emergency fund. Let's face it, we're not going to earn our way to wealth. That's a mistake many people make. We think that if we work harder, smarter, and longer, we'll achieve our financial dreams, but our paycheck alone, no matter how big it is, will not be the answer.

The last myth we'll discuss is unlike the others listed above. It's not the one that someone else has told you. It's the story you have told yourself that has kept you from investing in the stock market. It's time for a change and to break all your limits by discovering the lies we tell ourselves. What story have you been telling yourself about investing? What's stopping you from achieving financial freedom?

Are you telling yourself that it's too early to start, or too late, or you aren't making enough money to invest in the stock market?

Next time you hear one of these misconceptions about the stock market, you'll be able to weigh it against your knowledge. There is one consistent line of messaging many can agree on, which is putting money into the stock market over time can help build real wealth. As humans, this hyper-focus on the news of the moment can be damaging to our long-term success. We're tempted to concentrate not on a lifetime investing plan but on whether we should invest now or after the market rebounds.

I encourage investors to invest for lifetime financial goals, but many make decisions based on current news. This quote from Nick Murray says it best: *"Perspective reminds us that a multi-decade investment policy can only be rationally based on a multi-decade stock market history and that we must make our investment policy based on history, rather than headlines—or if you prefer, "the truth" rather than (the news)."* I love this quote because history has proven that long-term optimism remains the only realistic option and is undefeated.

Here is a fun exercise that can keep investors disciplined. When you start thinking about your current investments, look at the value of the stock market on the day you were born and then look at its value today. For example, the S&P 500, which is a stock market index tracking the stock performance of 500 large companies, shows the average price was $118.71 in 1980, and the average closing price was $4,111.76 by December 2022. In other words, if you invested $8,000 in the S&P 500 stock market in 1980, it would be nominally worth $798,165.88 in 2022.[1] These numbers aren't adjusted for inflation, so

1   www.in2013dollars.com/us/inflation/1980?amount=8000)

it's considered nominal. Several headline news and disasters occurred between 1980 and 2022, but they didn't shake the multi-decade investment plans.

If the dough rises the longer you keep it in the oven, why do we always hear about the quick returns on investments? We all have that friend who says, "You should invest in XYZ company because I've already made XXX dollars by investing in it." It's not so popular to say you're investing for a return you can pull out in 25 years. That's why we don't hear others bragging about it often. It doesn't gain applause from the audience. The social harmfulness of bragging about stock purchases is dysfunctional. It can cause the markets to swing in unexpected directions. For example, if I tell you how great my stock purchase is, and you decide to buy, I've just influenced the market, but it might not be a good buy. The more people buy, the more the stock appreciates in value. So, beware of others who brag about stock purchases because they might not fit lifetime investing plans. Some might suggest that bragging to others can satisfy the motive to craft and maintain a certain self-image.

There will always be risks with investing in the stock market, like most things in life. If you want to invest without any risk, the stock market isn't for you. Sometimes those risks are minimal, as with Treasury bonds (T-bonds). **In general, the more risk the investor is willing to take, the more potential for higher returns.** It's important to understand the threats involved with investing so you can try to avoid them. There are many risks, and below are the four major risks of investing in the stock market.

1. Company risk is the most popular for investors who purchase individual stocks. You can lose money if you invest in a company that fails to produce enough profit. You've heard the old saying,

"Don't put all your eggs in one basket." Another term for it is called business risk. It's anything that could threaten a company's financial health or lead to insolvency. Insolvency happens to companies that can no longer pay their bills. We've all been there at some point in our lives. Company risk can be reduced by analyzing quarterly earnings results, listening to management commentary on those results, and measuring performance with different financial ratios, which we will learn later in this book. But really, who is going to do all of that research when having all the public research in the world still won't turn you into a psychic by knowing what the future holds?

Although it is not guaranteed, diversification is the most efficient way to eliminate company risk. Consider buying other stocks across different industries in case things don't go according to plan. For example, if a farmer were to stumble while bringing a basket of eggs back from the henhouse, they could end up in a messy situation. Don't chance your breakfast and get it ruined by only having one farmer. Having multiple farmers, from various locations, delivering numerous items in addition to eggs, such as bacon and potatoes. All of these features combined will reduce the risk of having your breakfast ruined. Diversification includes owning stocks from several different industries, countries, and risk profiles, as well as other investments.

2. Market risk is what we're currently experiencing in 2022. No matter how great a company shines, its stock is still subject to the volatility of stock market risk. Remember stock prices are determined by supply and demand. If people are pulling money out of the stock market, the result would be stock prices falling. Market risk comes from movements in stock prices, interest rates, and exchange rates. In other words, the risk of losing money due to those above factors affects the overall performance of the financial markets. How do you prepare yourself when the stock market is down? Market downsides will happen on occasion, but history tells us that they're only temporary. A way to limit market risk is to ensure you have a source of cash outside of your investments for emergencies like market crashes. History tells us that down markets should only be temporary. For those in search of optimism during down markets, remember the birthday exercise we previously discussed.

3. Opportunity cost is the risk of missing out. It refers to gains you could have attained by choosing a different investment. If you don't put yourself in a position to achieve responsible investment growth, you risk leaving money on the table. It's best to pair your investment with your risk tolerance. Again, the more risk the investor is willing to take, the more potential for higher returns. What the Joneses had to sacrifice to live in a beautiful house might not be what you're willing to sacrifice. You can't compare their mansion to your apartment because they have a greater risk of losing their mansion tomorrow.

4. Liquidity risk is usually the most underestimated risk. It refers to how fast an investment can be sold for cash. Cash is the most liquid asset. Sometimes assets in 401(k)s and IRAs (Individual Retirement Accounts) might only be available to you after paying an early withdrawal penalty. If you're going to hold illiquid investments, make sure you have enough liquidity elsewhere in your plan to meet your potential needs. Most stocks are highly liquid, whereas real estate and private business ownership are on the other end of the spectrum.

There's no such thing as a risk-free stock or business, so if someone tells you differently, run. Although stocks face universal risks, the rewards of investing can still far outweigh the risk. As an investor, it's best to know the risks before entering the stock market and perhaps keep a stress ball near you to help during periods of market downturns. Spend some time thinking about these risks. You may discover that your tolerance for risk is lower than you expected or that you'll need to adjust to accepting more risk to meet your financial goals.

Summary:

The stock market has long been favored by banks, large corporations, and wealthy individuals, but misconceptions about how it works can lead to misunderstanding and inaccurate information. Common misconceptions are that investing in the stock market is like gambling, you can time the market, it's too complicated and time-consuming, it's only for the rich, and it's safer to keep money in a savings account. In reality, investing in the stock market can help build real wealth over the long term, and with the emergence of zero-commission online brokers and robo-advisors, it's available to anyone.

Risks involved with investing include company risk, market risk, opportunity cost, and liquidity risk. It's important to understand these risks and have a plan in place to manage them, as well as have emergency savings. Rather than trying to pick the perfect time to buy and sell, the best route for long-term success may be to plan and stay the course.

Action Steps:

1. Analyze quarterly earnings results for individual stocks.

2. Monitor different financial ratios to measure performance.

3. Diversify investments across different industries, countries, and risk profiles.

4. Have a source of cash outside of investments for emergencies.

5. Spend time understanding risks before entering the stock market.

CHAPTER 2
Roots of Money

You hear people say money is the root of all evil often. This can be true for people who speak it because words have power and can shape their beliefs. When we're conditioned to believe something early on, we tend to find examples to support our beliefs. Determination to prove your point can lead you to search for supporting evidence to back it up. I believe it's better to focus on the positive things money does for others. Money is an object with no intrinsic value. It's neither good nor bad. However, *how* people spend money may be considered good or bad.

Many wealthy people are the most generous and donate large sums of their money to charities and those less fortunate. Typically, those who say money is evil do not give any of their money away. They buy lottery tickets and enter every money competition possible. If they won, would they become evil as well? Many wealthy individuals got there because they were providing tremendous value to others, so it's important not to generalize.

In my last book *Wealth Building for Beginners*, I discussed how wealthy people aren't evil and poor people aren't holy. There are good and bad people in both categories. Those without money must not talk negatively about their circumstances because the more negative you get about a subject, the less likely you will ever attain it. I believe everyone can do far better for themselves and for others with money. Money can be used for good or desired for all the wrong reasons. I hope everyone reading this book is choosing to have money and choosing to do good with it. "Money is the root of all evil" is a misquote from the original, which is "The love of money is the root of all evil." Two very different things.

How did the concept of money start? Out of the desire to have goods, people traded items dating back to 600 BCE with King Alyattes of Lydia. The bartering conversations may have gone: "I want one of your weapons, can I trade you some of my animal skins?" Trading increased the speed of society's businesses and skill set because survival depended on having something of value to exchange with others. What if the weapon's owner didn't want any animal skins? A three-way currency needed to be created to provide both parties with a mutually desirable medium of exchange. This is how the first currency was developed; however, the trading system spread across the world and still survives today in some parts of the globe. There have been hundreds of currencies over the years from cows to salt to coins to paper to plastic, including the 162 official currencies worldwide.

Now instead of trading cows, people buy and sell shares in companies to profit from price changes, which is called stock trading. Let's get into the basics. What exactly are stocks and bonds? Imagine I own a restaurant near your house called Eddie's Chicken and Grits. My business is doing very well. Sales are going up, and our Facebook page has many likes. To ensure my business runs well, I need to pay for my employees, inventory, operations management, marketing, gas and electric, store lease, accountants, lawyers, and so on. While my profits are currently covering my expenses, I'm looking into opening another Eddie's Chicken and Grits since a second restaurant will help me increase profits and decrease overall expenses. However, my finance team stated I would need an additional $500,000, which I don't have.

Since I don't have the money, I asked my friend Leroy the barber to help me, but he's broke. So, I decided to go to the general public to help me with my restaurant. Before I spread the news that I need money to open my business, I must think about what I can offer them in return because there is no such thing as a free lunch.

The most basic options are: (one) ask the public to lend me money and pay them back interest for the loan in return, or (two) give them a partnership in my company. That is the difference between stocks and bonds. Bonds are loans given to the issuer, and they agree to pay you back the full loan or face value on a specific date, plus periodic interest payments along the way twice a year. Stocks are equity in a company which means you are a part owner. A single share of the stock means fractional ownership of the company, which is different from bonds because once you pay the principal back along with the interest payments, the relationship ends. Both stocks and bonds help companies raise money, either through equity in ownership or offering debt in loans. An investor who buys a corporate bond is lending money to the company. An investor who buys stock is buying an ownership share of the company.

The term "securities" are broadly defined as financial instruments that hold value and can be traded between parties. This catch-all term is for investments you can buy or sell, such as stocks or bonds. Other securities are tradable financial instruments.

"Investing should be more like watching paint dry or watching grass grow. If you want excitement, take $800 and go to Las Vegas." – Paul Samuelson

The stock market was created because companies have been collecting funds from willing investors to support all types of businesses. To understand how the stock market works, let's go back to my example of listing Eddie's Chicken and Grits on the stock market to raise capital. First, I will advertise my company to a group of top investors. If these investors like my idea and can envision expanding Eddie's Chicken and Grits, they will receive the first dibs at investing in my company and will sponsor our initial public offering (IPO).

An IPO puts a business on the public market where anyone who believes it will be profitable could buy shares of my stock. As mentioned earlier, buying stocks makes those investors partial owners. Shares purchased could jump-start the company's growth, and later more investors might want to drink the Kool-Aid because the company is growing. As the demand for the stock increases, so does the price of the stock, which will also raise the value of the stocks people already own. It spreads like wildfire. Now I'm showing off how many people are buying my stock to other potential buyers because this helps build public confidence and my market value with getting funding for other company initiatives later.

Eddie's Chicken and Grits is now doing well in the stock market. But what if someone finds a cockroach in their food at one of my restaurants? My company might start becoming less profitable, and the reverse can happen in which my market value and stock price decrease. It can decrease just as fast as it increased. If investors think my stock will decline, they will sell their stocks with the hopes of selling it for more than they paid for it before my company loses more value. The faster my stock price decreases, the faster investors lose money unless my company becomes profitable again.

These fluctuations in market value and stock price can go on for years. Numerous variables can cause day-to-day noise in the market, causing market fluctuations (e.g., company news and performance), economic factors (e.g., interest rate shifts and inflation, industry trends, market sentiment, which is the general attitude of investors toward a stock), and unexpected events like natural disasters. This is another reason why long-term investing is generally more reliable; you aren't reacting to the day-to-day noise of investors trying to make quick cash.

With all of this trading going on, another medium of exchange nearly broke the internet since it was getting traded so much. It's called cryptocurrency. Many people were trading it and didn't even know what it was. I couldn't have been the only person who had no idea what cryptocurrency was until further research. At one point it was the third most searched term on Google in 2018. Let's translate what cryptocurrency is into plain English.

We discussed what money is and how it represents value. If I wanted some of your weapons, but you did not want any of my animal skin, I would have to give you a three-way currency that serves as a medium of exchange, which is money. Over the years, money has taken many different forms like cows, salt, wheat, seashells, gold, paper, etc. These things all represent value, but in order for something to stay valuable, people have to trust that it will remain valuable long enough for them to redeem that value in the future.

Before banks, we always trusted in something to represent value, but then we changed our beliefs from trusting in something to trusting in someone.

Over time, people found it too difficult to handle cows or other forms of money, such as gold, so paper money was invented. It worked like this: a bank or government would take your gold and give you receipt certificates, which we call dollar bills. Bills were much easier to carry than gold, salt, or any other currency. If you ever wanted your gold back, you would simply take your bills back to the bank in exchange for your gold.

Eventually, people started trading only paper bills, leaving all the gold bars in the bank because it's much more practical and convenient. These bills were backed by the bank and the government's promise that they were worth the same as gold, which were kept in the bank's vaults. Even though people couldn't see the physical gold, they trusted the government, so this continued to work with bills. This is how fiat money started, which is a national currency not tied to the price of a commodity, such as gold. The value of fiat money is largely based on the public's faith in the currency's issuer, which is the government or central bank.

Fiat money has two main downsides: it's centralized and not limited by quantity. A centralized authority like the government or central bank controls and issues it. Not limited by quantity means the government or central bank can print as much money as they want, which devalues existing money already owned. When you're flooding the market with more money, the value of each dollar drops. Some might argue that inflation is very high in 2022 because of the disaster relief loans and Paycheck Protection Program (PPP) loans issued to stabilize the economy during the pandemic. Soon after fiat money was in place, we moved to digital money because it was easier for the regulators to keep track of what people own. Digital money refers to credit cards, wire transfers, PayPal, Cash App, Zelle, Venmo, etc. The amount of physical money in the world is drastically shrinking.

How does digital money actually work? If I have a file that represents a dollar, what's stopping me from copying it a million times? This problem is so common that it has its own name—the "double spend problem." The bank's solution is to keep a ledger on their computer that keeps track of who owns what. Everyone has an account, and this ledger keeps a tally for each account. We trust the bank and the bank trusts its systems. **Whenever you give someone control over the money supply, you're giving them lots of power, which can create problems like corruption and mismanagement.** When you give away control of your money, you trust it will be handled well and your accounts won't get frozen or stolen. We have all heard of scandals with corrupt banks that mismanaged money.

In October 2008, everything changed when Satoshi Nakamoto published a document proposing a system for decentralized currency. This system claims to create a digital currency that solves the double spending problem but without the need for a central authority like banks. This was the birth of cryptocurrency! It's a transparent ledger without a central authority controlling it. For example, since most money today is already digital, the bank manages its ledger of customer transactions, but it isn't transparent for everyone to see.

If I make a purchase from you with my credit card, you cannot see if I have sufficient money until you run it through a system that connects with my bank. You can't look at the bank's ledger on their computers. Only the bank has complete control over it.

Cryptocurrency has transparent ledgers so that anyone can see all of the balances taking place. However, you will not know who owns these balances because it's anonymous. It's open, transparent, and trackable.

Cryptocurrency is also decentralized because there isn't one computer that holds its ledger. With cryptocurrency, every computer that participates in the system also keeps a copy of the ledger, which is called the "blockchain." If computer hackers wanted to overtake this system, they would have to take down thousands of computers that maintain copies of the same codes with constant updates.

Cryptocurrency isn't a physical currency; there are only rows of transactions and balances. Since digital money came into existence, we now have an alternative to fiat money. A cryptocurrency is a form of money that no bank or government controls. Cryptocurrency cuts a lot of the middlemen from the process of transferring money, making transaction fees cheaper. When you own cryptocurrency, you own the right to access a specific address record in the ledger and send funds from it to a different address. There you have it. You know more than most people about cryptocurrency.

Cryptocurrency is very risky and considered a highly speculative investment since supply and demand drive its volatility. This means it's subject to astonishing price swings, with big gains followed by enormous losses, and sometimes all within a matter of hours. I generally don't prefer discussing speculative investments in wealth-building strategies, but cryptocurrency remains a popular question mark.

Summary:

People often say that money is the root of all evil, but this is a misquote of the original phrase, "The love of money is the root of all evil." Money is neither good nor bad, but how people spend it can be seen as good or bad. Wealthy people are often the most generous with their money, giving away huge amounts to charities and those in need. Negative attitudes toward money can prevent people from ever having it, and there are good and bad people in both the wealthy and poor categories.

Eddie's Chicken and Grits is an example of a business that needed additional funding for growth, and this is where the stock market comes in. Stocks and bonds are two types of securities companies can use to raise money, either through equity ownership or debt loans. Cryptocurrency is a decentralized form of digital money, with transparent ledgers and no central authority controlling it. It's a highly speculative investment with high levels of risk and volatility.

Action Steps:

1. Research the original quote, "The love of money is the root of all evil," to understand the true meaning.

2. Replace negative beliefs about money with positive ones in order to attract wealth.

3. Consider how money can be used for good and focus on its potential for positive change.

4. Learn about stocks, bonds, and cryptocurrencies to understand how businesses can raise funds.

5. Understand the risks associated with investing in cryptocurrencies, and research a variety of strategies for mitigating risk.

CHAPTER 3
Why Invest in the Stock Market?

Wwhen you purchase real estate, do you watch the value of your property go up and down every day? Home values can go up and down every day, just like the stock market. The biggest difference between real estate and the stock market is that real estate is tangible. You can touch the brick-and-mortar. This typically gives us emotional comfort. I've never had to answer the question, "Why invest in real estate?" from others, but I've often had to answer the question of "Why invest in the stock market?" Similar to the stock market, there are zero guarantees in real estate.

One of the reasons why we're more comfortable with real estate is because we're more familiar with its long-term tracking throughout history. We grew up with it. We've lived in these neighborhoods since we were kids. Most people should be able to do the same with the stock market, but the challenge is learning something new that you don't understand. Some mutual funds have an 80-year history with only a handful of down years with an average rate of return of 11%.

An annual rate of return of 11% for 80 years, some might argue, is much safer statistically than your rental property.

I want everyone to be knowledgeable about the stock market. The Bible says, "My people are destroyed from lack of knowledge" (Hosea 4:6). As I mentioned in the introduction, knowledge gives you calmness, which is why I can fly in an airplane without being overtaken by anxiety.

Investing in the stock market can help you build savings, protect your money from inflation and taxes, and maximize income. The primary reason most people invest in stocks is the potential return compared to alternatives, such as bank certificates of deposit (CDs), gold, treasury bonds, and more. The ability to earn passive income can be achieved with dividend stocks. Most dividend stocks pay quarterly dividends, but some companies pay monthly. Dividends can help supplement your paycheck or retirement income like social security.

One main reason why many prefer to invest in the stock market over real estate is because most stocks trade publicly on a major stock exchange, making it easy to buy and sell them. This makes stocks a more liquid investment compared to real estate, which you can't quickly sell. It's easier to buy and sell shares of stock than it is to list and sell a property. You can borrow against both investments, but it's easier to borrow against stocks. With the stock market, you can achieve diversification by building a portfolio across many different industries. It also offers the opportunity to start small for those who don't have much money.

The very first step to investing is to determine your investment goals. When I ask someone what their investment goals are, I often hear that they want to make more money. This isn't an investment goal. **Investment goals provide structure and purpose to the money you put aside for investment products. Saying that your goal with investing is to make more money is like saying your retirement goal is to be happy.** There's no structure or direction. Some investors know what their goals are, while others need a framework.

Is your goal to significantly grow your money? Do you want to rely on investments to generate a steady income? Do you want to focus on preserving your principal? Do you want to risk it all on an opportunity for very large gains? Once you know your goals or investment objectives, you can either choose a portfolio or have a professional design a portfolio around those guidelines. As mentioned, all investments have risk, and the higher the risk, the higher the reward.

Another important guideline for your portfolio is to manage your risk tolerance. Risk tolerance measures the degree of loss you're willing to endure in your portfolio. Many people might want to be billionaires, but many might not want to sacrifice time, family, notoriety, stress, or freedom. If your goal is to significantly grow your money, but you're willing to risk very little, then you must evaluate those factors. By definition, you're a conservative growth investor seeking consistent maximum growth with a relatively modest degree of risk. I don't want to complicate things that can be very simple. Below are the basic definitions for the different investment objectives and risk tolerance:

Investment Objectives

Income investors - Seeking maximum amount of income given their risk tolerance and willingness to give up capital appreciation and growth of income in order to seek a higher level of current income.

Growth and Income investors - Seeking current income but also seeking both income and capital growth over time. These investors are willing to give up a portion of their current income in order to provide for potential future growth.

Growth investors - Are not currently seeking income; their primary objective is capital appreciation.

Speculation investors - Seeking maximum return through a broad range of investment strategies, which involves a high level of risk, including the potential for significant loss of principal.

Capital preservation investors - Seeking protection of the monetary value of your investment. Is not concerned with this investment growing larger, but if it does then that is icing on the cake.

Risk Tolerances

Conservative: A conservative investor values protecting the principal over seeking appreciation. This investor is comfortable accepting lower returns for a higher degree of liquidity and/or stability. Typically, a conservative investor primarily seeks to minimize risk and loss of principal.

Moderately Conservative: A moderately conservative investor values principal preservation but is comfortable accepting a small degree of risk and volatility to seek some degree of appreciation. This investor desires greater liquidity, is willing to accept lower returns, and is willing to accept minimal losses.

Moderate: A moderate investor values reducing risks and enhancing returns equally. This investor is willing to accept modest risks to seek higher long-term returns. A Moderate investor may endure a short-term loss of principal and a lower degree of liquidity in exchange for long-term appreciation.

Moderate Growth: A moderate growth investor values higher long-term returns and is willing to accept considerable risk. This investor is comfortable with short-term fluctuations in exchange for seeking long-term appreciation. The Moderate Growth investor is willing to endure larger short-term losses of principal in exchange for the potential of higher long-term returns. Liquidity is a secondary concern to a Moderate Growth investor.

Moderately Aggressive: A moderately aggressive investor primarily values higher long-term returns and is willing to accept significant risk. This investor believes higher long-term returns are more important than protecting the principal. A Moderately Aggressive investor may endure large losses in favor of potentially higher long-term returns. Liquidity may not be a concern to a Moderately Aggressive investor.

Aggressive: An aggressive investor values maximizing returns and is willing to accept substantial risk. This investor believes maximizing long-term returns is more important than protecting the principal. An aggressive investor may endure extensive volatility and significant losses. Liquidity is generally not a concern to an aggressive investor.

Pick one of these categories from both lists and that will tell you exactly what type of investor you are.

The stock market is a fantastic way to build wealth, as shown in my popular book, *Wealth Building for Beginners*, but it's not the only way to invest. There are alternative investments that don't trade in the stock market. An alternative investment is often classified as any asset other than stocks, bonds, or cash. Alternative investments can have a low correlation to the stock market and may perform better when the stock market is down. It's one of the most dynamic asset classes that cover a wide range of investments with unique characteristics. Popular alternative investments are real estate, real estate investment trusts, gold and silver, managed futures, and collectibles. Of course, real estate is the most popular alternative investment. Buying a residential or commercial property to rent out can be profitable. Reliable tenants can generate consistent income, and your expenses are mostly limited to maintenance and repairs.

If you want to own real estate but not manage it, a real estate investment trust (REIT) might be a great option. Owning rental properties comes with costs and hidden fees, such as vacancies, capital expenses, and the time value of your work. REITs offer you the benefit of being a landlord but avoiding the major downside, like holding a less liquid asset. REITs are companies that own a basket of real estate across a range of property sectors that pay regular income to investors.

So rent is paid from that basket of real estate; they pay the pool of investors a portion of the rent payment. Gold and silver are classic investments that are highly prized possessions that will probably remain in high demand for most industries. Unlike other investments susceptible to inflation, gold and silver don't have that problem. It's a generational investment that is highly liquid compared to other investments. My dad used to purchase several gold jewelry, which he considered his emergency saving plan. When times get hard, he would pawn his gold jewelry at the pawn shop. I don't recommend this strategy, but it worked for my dad.

Managed futures is a strategy whereby an account professional assembles a diversified basket of futures contracts. A futures contract is an agreement to buy or sell an underlying asset at a later date for a predetermined price. This sounds confusing, but it's quite simple. To better understand futures, think about how the price for a box of Kellogg's corn flakes normally stays the same even though the crops, such as the corn that makes it, fluctuates in price depending on the season. A box of corn flakes doesn't cost more in February and March, but corn does. Corn flakes will have stable pricing thanks to the futures market.

The futures markets allow the people who sell and buy large quantities, such as corn, to protect themselves from price jumps without Kellogg's going out of business. Instead of Kellogg's and the farmer buying and selling corn, they buy and sell the contracts. The contract will allow Kellogg's to buy corn in the future at a locked-in price, ensuring they will be able to purchase corn for the same price further down the road. A forward price was determined today. Once the parties enter a futures contract, they're obligated to carry out the transaction of the underlying asset in the future at the delivery date, no matter how profitable or unprofitable it ends up being. These contracts can be bought or sold on the market without the underlying asset ever changing hands.

Collectibles include a wide range of things, including wine, vintage cars, art, stamps, coins, baseball cards, etc. Some of you might be thinking, *I purchased this book to learn about investments and he's writing about baseball cards.* Yes, classic baseball cards are an alternative investment to the stock market that can be very profitable. The current record price for a 1952 Mickey Mantle baseball card is over 12 million dollars. I'm just saying…

Earned income can never compare to the power of compounding! Many people go through a vicious life loop of work, get the money, spend the money, work, get the money, spend the money. You must move from just working for money to a world where money works for you. The goal is to step out of that loop and walk the path to financial freedom. The way to start on that path is to make a decision to tap into the great power of compounding. Albert Einstein once said, "Compound interest is the eighth wonder of the world. He who understands it earns it; he who doesn't, pays it." If you double one penny each day continuously over 30 days, how much will you have?"

Compound interest is when you earn interest on both the money you've saved and the interest you earn. Compound interest can significantly boost investment returns over the long term. Simple interest is interest paid only on the principal. That is how not understanding compound interest can cost you. For example, installment loans, like auto loans and mortgages, use simple interest. The smaller the principal, the smaller the interest. Credit cards and student loan debt typically use compounding interest. This means you will have more interest the further the life of the loan continues. The less you pay off your original loan balance, the more the total amount (principal plus interest) owed accumulates because of interest.

This book is about education only and not advisory, but I can't help but write this: Stop dragging on credit card debt! Let compounding interest work in your favor and not against you. Let's say you start investing in your 20s a monthly amount of $100, and you gain a return of 1% a month, which is 12% annually. You continue investing the same amount and receiving the same return for 40 years. Your high school bestie Greg is the same age as you, and you both plan to retire at the same time, but Greg doesn't start investing until 30 years after you started.

Now retirement is approaching, and Greg only has ten years left to invest, so he decided to invest $1,000 a month while averaging the same return of 1% a month. When you approach your 40-year savings point and your bestie Greg has only saved for 10 years, Greg will have accumulated $230,000, while you have accumulated north of $1.17 million. Despite Greg saving 10 times as much as you, the power of compounded interest made your pockets 5 times greater than his.

Now let's see how much you will earn if you double one penny every day for 30 days.

Compound Interest

Einsteins 8th Wonder of the World

Watch what happens to this penny over 30 days.

Day	Amount	Day	Amount
Day 1	$.01	Day 16	$327.68
Day 2	$.02	Day 17	$655.36
Day 3	$.04	Day 18	$1,310.72
Day 4	$.08	Day 19	$2,621.44
Day 5	$.16	Day 20	$5,242.88
Day 6	$.32	Day 21	$10,485.76
Day 7	$.64	Day 22	$20,971.52
Day 8	$1.28	Day 23	$41,943.04
Day 9	$2.56	Day 24	$83,886.08
Day 10	$5.12	Day 25	$167,772.16
Day 11	$10.24	Day 26	$335,544.32
Day 12	$20.48	Day 27	$671,088.64
Day 13	$40.96	Day 28	$1,342,177.28
Day 14	$81.92	Day 29	$2,684,354.56
Day 15	$163.84	Day 30	$5,368,709.12

Many have heard the term bull and bear markets, but where does its name come from, and how do they impact your investment decisions? An early mention of bull and bear appeared in the 1769 edition of Thomas Mortimer's book *Every Man His Own Broker*, and we have been using these terms ever since. A bull market happens when securities are on the rise, while a bear market is the opposite. These terms describe how stock markets are performing in general and derived from how each animal attacks its enemy. A bull will ram its horns up in the air, like a bullfight, and a bear will swipe its claws down.

While investors may be more willing to buy during a bullish market, a bearish market will likely lead them to sell. And although it's important to understand the direction of the markets, it's very difficult to predict when the change will come from bull to bear and vice versa. Remember, the best strategy for managing market risk is by building long-term strategies and not trying to time the market.

Chapter Summary:

While the stock market is a great way to build wealth, it's not the only way to invest. Alternative investments such as real estate, REITs, gold and silver, managed futures, and collectibles are all popular options. These all offer low correlation to the stock market and may perform better when the stock market is down. It's important to understand your investment goals and risk tolerance, as well as the basics of different types of investments, so you can determine the best route for your financial future. Bull and bear markets are terms used to describe the general performance of the stock market, and understanding the market's direction can help you make educated decisions when investing. Ultimately, the best strategy for managing market risk is to build long-term strategies and not try to time the market.

Action Steps:

1. Understand the meaning of bull and bear markets, and how they impact your investment decisions.

2. Research the history of the terms, and why they have been used for centuries.

3. Create a long-term investment strategy to manage market risk.

4. Consider both the bullish and bearish markets when making decisions.

5. Reevaluate your strategy regularly to ensure it's still aligned with your needs.

CHAPTER 4

How Much Can the Stock Market Fall in a Day?

The stock market can be considered a representation of how the world reacts at any given moment. Its data is an exact imprint of a specific moment. Viewers get to learn what the world is thinking and feeling and what it will do next. *I'm not sure about the stock market, but I'll still invest, and if I see the value of my portfolio slightly decreasing, I will sell my shares and take all my money.* It seems like it would be easy.

The problem is no one gets a calendar to get alerted of the time, nature, and projected magnitude of future drops in the market. It can happen at any time. No one likes to lose money, so the tendency is to hold off as long as you can before reacting, but sometimes it can spiral downward just as quickly as it accelerates up.

In September 1929, the Dow Jones Industrial Average stock market reached an all-time high, but in the very next month, October 24, 1929, stocks began to fall. The following Monday and Tuesday, known as Black Tuesday, the market lost 25% of its value, which was the start of the Great Depression.

Can you imagine losing a quarter of your retirement savings after one weekend when it took you decades to build it? It's every investor's worst nightmare—a sudden market decline that wipes out years of gains in a matter of days.

The S&P 500 stock market has been down double digits eleven times total, not counting the year 2022. Below are the years and possible causes:

1931	-42.8%	Great Depression
2008	-36.6%	Great Financial Crisis
1937	-35.3%	1937 Crash
1974	-25.9%	1973-74 Bear Market
1930	-25.1%	Great Depression
2002	-22.0%	Dot-Com Crash
1973	-14.3%	1973-74 Bear Market
1941	-12.8%	WWII
2001	-11.9%	Dot-Com Crash
1940	-10.7%	WWII
1957	-10.5%	1957-58 Recession

In other words, the worst years in the US stock market came during wars, market crashes, and sudden disruptions like economic bubbles. So much of the market is driven by emotion. Any one of these events could cause investors to sell off, and taking cues from each other, their panic rush to offload stocks intensifies. It might be seen as all three of these factors can cause high volumes and panic selling, which leads to snowballing declines.

A stock market crash is characterized by a decline of at least 10% over one or several days. It's a sharp, sudden drop in stock prices caused by a variety of reasons. The largest stock market crash happened on October 19, 1987. The stock markets fell by 22% in one day! This is known as Black Monday—the largest percentage of stock market drop in a single day. Normally, stock indexes typically charge between -1% and 1% on any single day. Anything outside of these parameters could be considered alarming for better or worse. Since we had a look at some of the worst years in the stock market, let's review some of the worst market crashes. A market crash doesn't automatically mean a down year. Remember, market crashes are intense drops within a few days.

Some of the most popular stock market crashes are:

The Great Depression Crash of 1929 – This was the first major US market crash.

The Black Monday Crash of October 1987 – This was attributed to computer trading.

The Dot-Com Crash of 2000-01 – Similar to the crash of 87', this collapse was triggered by technology stocks.

Stock Market Crash of 2007-08 – Many might remember movies about this one such as *The Big Short*. Triggered by the collapse of mortgage-backed securities in the housing sector.

The COVID Crash of March 2020 – The pandemic impacted many sectors. Triggered by the government's reaction to the COVID-19 outbreak.

The S&P 500 origin goes back to 1923, and we reviewed eleven double-digit down years and a handful of market crashes in 100 years. What about all of the great years when fortunes were made? Like learning the worst that could happen while flying in an airplane, learning the worst about the stock market made me feel much better! Most years the stock market gives investors double-digit returns. From 1928 to 2018, the S&P 500 has shown 66 calendar-year gains and 24 losses over a 90-year period. That means stocks have advanced roughly three out of four years. During that period, the annualized return was 9.6%. Of course, averages never tell the whole story, and calendar year returns are rarely average in the stock market because we discussed crashes and bull runs. Of those 66 positive annual gains, the average return was roughly 21%. And 51 of those 66 years saw double-digit returns.

Since the largest stock market crashes, there have been measures aimed at helping markets find their bearings during exceedingly choppy times and can help prevent a drastic downward freefall of the market. The stock market cannot completely bottom out in one day because of procedures called circuit breakers. On October 19, 1987, the first circuit breaker was put into place. Circuit breakers are temporary trading pauses imposed in the stock market if a severe market price decline happens on the same day. Exactly as its name suggests, standard electrical circuit breakers are critical safety mechanisms in any home that cuts the flow of power in the event of a "surge."

The same concepts exist in the stock market. Pause during times of excess volatility or heavy emotion-driven trading to prevent more downward price drops. Trading in the entire stock market is put on pause in the event of a circuit breaker. These mechanisms serve as a brief "time-out" for investors to step back and get a grip. The primary function of circuit breakers is to slow momentum and let things cool off for a moment.

"Occasionally, buying or selling momentum comes so fast and furious that the relationships between the indices and their individual components get askew. Circuit breakers help slow this momentum and get the relationships back in line, which allows stability in the market."_ JJ Kinahan, chief market strategist at TD Ameritrade.

There are different levels of circuit breakers. The level 1 circuit-breaker activates when the S&P 500 falls by 7% from the previous day at any time before 3:45 pm EST. Trading will pause for 15 minutes. The level 2 circuit breaker activates when the S&P 500 falls by 13% from the prior day at any time before 3:45 pm EST. Trading will pause for another 15 minutes. The level 3 circuit breaker activates when the S&P 500 falls by 20% from the prior day at any time. Trading will stop for the rest of the day.

To help visualize how the stock market works, think about a standard flea market. You have a group of buyers and sellers coming together that forms the market. An easy way to think about the stock market is to consider it as a network of stock exchanges where traders and investors buy and sell shares of publicly traded companies. If trading on any given day gets negatively out of control, there will be a circuit breaker. The stock market opens at 9:30 am EST on business days and closes at 4:00 pm EST. Just like security opens, pauses, and closes a flea market; the Securities and Exchange Commission (SEC) are the ones who regulate the stock market.

This book is to be read like a workbook and not a novel. We've learned a lot thus far in just four short chapters. Please answer the questions below, so I know that you're with me before moving on to more complex discussions. If you're struggling to answer the questions below, please reread chapters one through four. It's better to be slow and careful in the right direction than to be fast and careless on the wrong path.

Review:

1. What is a stock market, and how does it work?

2. What are the four major risks of investing?

3. What was the value of the stock market when you were born, and what is it today?

4. How did the concept of money begin?

5. What is cryptocurrency?

6. What are the goals and risk tolerance of investors investing in the stock market?

7. What is compounded interest?

8. What are alternative investments outside of the stock market?

9. What are bull and bear markets?

10. What are measures to prevent the stock markets from drastic large percentage drops in one day?

Summary:

The stock market is a network of exchanges where traders and investors buy and sell shares of publicly traded companies. It's driven by emotion and can lead to intense drops within days, known as market crashes. The worst market crashes in the US have been during wars, market crashes, and economic bubbles. The largest crash, known as Black Monday, was in 1987 when the market dropped 22% in one day.

In order to prevent a drastic downward freefall of the market, circuit breakers are put in place, which are temporary trading pauses that occur when the stock market has experienced a severe decline. The stock market can be risky but has seen 66 calendar-year gains and 24 losses over a 90-year period with an annualized return of 9.6%. Investors should consider their goals and risk tolerance when investing in the stock market, as well as understand the concept of money and alternative investments such as cryptocurrency.

Action Steps:

1. Understand the psychology of the stock market and the data it provides.

2. Invest cautiously and be aware of the potential for sudden drops in the market.

3. Learn the worst that could happen in the stock market and be prepared.

4. Understand the function of circuit breakers and how they can help prevent drastic downward freefalls.

5. Understand the concept of a stock market, how it works, and the goals and risk tolerance of investors.[2,3]

---

2   National Bureau of Economic Research
3   A Wealth of Common Sense by Ben Carlson, CFA

CHAPTER 5

Characteristics of Stocks, Bonds, Mutual Funds, Index Funds, and ETFs

N ow that you understand how the stock market works, where do you begin if you're ready to start investing? Investing can be overwhelming because there are many investments to choose from. The most basic investments are stocks, bonds, mutual funds, and exchange-traded funds (ETFs). There are parallels between playing golf and understanding the stock market. The field would resemble the stock market. Sometimes bad weather can steer your ball in unfavorable directions. Your target is the holes. You know exactly where you want the ball to go, like your goals with investment. The clubs are your investments. Some golf clubs make the ball travel further and faster, but you don't use the driver if you're close to the hole. You might not want to invest everything in stocks if you're a few years away from retirement. I'll explain that sentence more as we get further into the chapter.

Stocks, bonds, mutual funds, and ETFs are the basic investments that drive you to your goals. They are the tools you use to build the house. When do you use the hammer, screwdriver, or wrench? Just as it's important to know how each tool works and what job each is best suited for in building a house, it's imperative to know how each type of investment works best in building your portfolio.

When an investor buys a stock, part ownership in the form of a share is purchased. If the company does well, the investor benefits by seeing an increase in the value of the share. The share can either be held or sold at a profit. If the company doesn't do well, the investor may lose some or all of the investment. There is no guarantee the company will do well, and we know the risk-reward relationship with investments. **Investing in stocks has the potential to earn much higher profits than bonds because stocks are riskier. The more profitable a company becomes, the more valuable its stock.**

The most common type of stock is called common stock. You have an ownership position in a company and usually have a vote in company issues. Another type of stock is called preferred stock. I don't want to get too in the weeds with this type of stock because it's not as "common." One main difference from common stock is that preferred stock comes with no voting rights. You can't vote on company issues at the annual meetings. It's called preferred because it gives investors a priority claim when a company pays dividends or distributes assets to shareholders.

A bond is an IOU, aka I owe you, from the company or issuer that promises to pay an investor interest over the life of the bond, plus repay the principal at a specific due date. OK, so let's back up. Stocks and bonds are what companies issue to raise money for their company. When Eddie's Chicken and Grits want to raise money for expansion, they can either issue stock to the public and offer an ownership stake in their company or ask for loans that are called bonds. The interest on the loans will be paid in intervals from the company to the investor twice a year, and the principal amount borrowed will be paid in its entirety at the end of the term.

I'm familiar with this concept because as a kid my dad used to borrow money from a loan shark.

My dad had to make periodic interest payments on the loan until he could repay its entirety. In this example, the loan shark is the investor, and my dad is the company. This is a way to invest while still minimizing risk. It can also ensure an income stream since bonds often pay interest twice a year. Some bonds also carry tax advantages, such as municipal bonds. These are bonds issued by a state or local government to help raise money for projects, such as the construction of highways, bridges, schools, etc. The government will give you a tax break if you invest in their bonds so they can gain more capital to execute projects that help the community. If you own a municipal bond, you're a creditor to the local government. Pretty cool, huh? The only problem is the government doesn't pay very much interest.

There are still risks involved with investing in bonds. While US savings bonds are considered one of the safest investments, bonds issued by individual companies may be risky if the company runs into financial difficulties. Bonds are still considered much safer than stocks and therefore are less risky.

What if Eddie's Chicken and Grits go bankrupt years later, but they have outstanding shares of stock that investors own (shares outstanding) and bonds owned by investors that the company hasn't paid back yet (bonds outstanding)? If an investor owns shares of a company's stock that declared bankruptcy, the investor will face a difficult decision: "Do I hang onto the shares, or do I cut my losses and attempt to sell my shares?"

It's very possible that a stock purchase can lose money and, in the worst-case scenario, the stock value could drop to zero. That is a decision an investor will have to make because shares of a company that files for bankruptcy are at heightened risk of falling to zero. On the flip side, there have been companies that have emerged from bankruptcy successfully, such as General Motors, Chrysler, Marvel Entertainment, and more. Even Apple was at one point in dire straits and on the verge of going bust in 1997, but they're soaring now.

The moral of the story is investing in stocks can be risky because, in the event of a bankruptcy, you could lose everything. However, if the company's stock value increases like Apple, you could also experience tremendous gains.

Bonds, on the other hand, offer more protection during bankruptcies than stocks. To help minimize the risks, laws are in place to protect you while also providing creditors with a portion of debt repayment. Chapter 7 and 11 of the federal bankruptcy laws govern how US companies go out of business or attempt to recover from financial hardship. When a company files for Chapter 7, it ceases operations and its assets are sold to repay creditors and investors, which are bondholders. The company must make every attempt to repay the principal to bondholders. Chapter 11 bankruptcy allows a company to reorganize in hopes of becoming profitable again.

Once a new plan is approved in court, the bankrupt company emerges as a newly organized company with less debt. While either type of bankruptcy often means a stockholder loses money, investors holding bonds are much more likely to recover at least part of the principal value. The laws that determine the hierarchy in which creditors are repaid consist of senior debt, subordinated debt, preferred equity, and lastly, common equity. What does this mean? Senior debt is simply the label placed on the debt (bonds), that takes priority over other debts. It's usually a debt secured by collateral, such as assets of the company, and these bonds must be paid off before any other debts when a company files for bankruptcy. Subordinated debt is unsecured bonds. You know what is preferred and common stock for chapter two. Equities are the same as stocks, which are shares in a company.

Mutual funds can be great options for beginners to start investing and building wealth. Mutual funds are types of financial accounts made up of a pool of money collected from many investors to invest in securities like money market instruments, stocks, bonds, and other assets. It's like investing in a basket of different securities. It can have lots of diversification. That basket is managed by investment professionals and money managers. They decide which securities to put in the basket to match the fund's objectives stated in its prospectus. A prospectus is a document that provides details about an investment offering to the public.

Remember, investing is the action or process of putting money to work to attempt to increase its value. The money manager's job is to organize the securities in the fund in such a way that can increase in value.

Mutual funds are great for beginners because investors gain access to professionally managed portfolios of stocks, bonds, and other securities. The average mutual fund holds over a hundred different securities, which means there's lots of diversification for a low price. It's like not putting all your eggs in one basket.

For example, consider an investor named Buckwheat who buys only Amazon stock before the company has a bad quarter. Buckwheat stands to lose a great deal of value because all his dollars are tied to one company. On the other side of the coin, a different investor named Mary Beth may buy shares of a mutual fund that happens to own some Amazon stock. When Amazon has a bad quarter, Mary Beth will lose significantly less because Amazon is just a small part of the fund's portfolio. Investing in mutual funds is a great way to begin your investing journey. Many professionals don't recommend investing in single stocks because there's too much risk in tying your investments to the performance of a handful of companies.

Mutual funds are the most common investment option offered in 401(k) plans. A 401(k) is an employer-sponsored plan that invests your money for retirement and is offered by for-profit companies. It's the most common employer-sponsored retirement vehicle that enables employees to make contributions that receive special tax considerations from their paychecks.

First off, the word 401(k) refers to section 401(k) of the US Tax Code that was enacted by Congress in 1978. Many 401(k) company providers offer an employer match, meaning the company will contribute an annual percentage of eligible employees' compensation to their 401(k) account. A popular structure is an employer matching 100% of what you put in, up to 6%, and then they don't match any more contributions after that amount. If you put in 4%, they will put in 4%, and if you put in 6%, they will put in 6%, however, if you put in 8%, they will only put in 6%.

So, let's simplify this with an example. Rosco works for a for-profit company called We Sell Stuff To Profit, which offers a 401(k) plan to its eligible employees. We Sell Stuff To Profit tells Rosco that they value him working there, so they will contribute one dollar into Rosco's bucket every time he puts one dollar into his bucket. Rosco puts one dollar in his bucket, and We Sell Stuff To Profit puts one dollar as well. This process will continue until We Sell Stuff To Profits says, "Alright Rosco, we have given you enough. You already have 6% of your contributions that we matched you dollar-for-dollar in your bucket because we appreciate you. Now if you want to continue putting in more money in your bucket, you can, up until the IRS limits will allow, but we're done for this pay period." Then, Rosco's bucket is dumped into the stock market for possible stock market returns. As illustrated, these plans are great incentives for the employee to save and build wealth.

Mutual funds, index funds, and ETFs are different in similar investment vehicles. Many people confuse these three investment vehicles. Mutual funds have been around the longest, the early 1900s to be exact. It was created so that several people can pull their money and make investments together.

Mutual funds offer three benefits:

1. Convenience. You get to own many different stocks all in one package. Without a mutual fund, you would have to spend time researching and buying all the individual stocks that one mutual fund could offer.

2. Diversification. You will own a lot of stocks all at once. One mutual fund normally offers over one hundred stocks.

3. **Professional Management**. Instead of researching all these companies on your own, you will have a skilled professional who does it for you.

Convenience and diversification are major benefits, but some might argue that having professional management is too expensive and cuts your bottom-line profit with fees. When some professional is picking the stocks for your mutual fund, this is called active management. Actively managed mutual funds are intended to beat a certain benchmark index. Actively managed mutual funds generally charge between 1% and 2% of annual fees because the smart guys have to get paid. Even if the fund manager makes poor investment decisions and your account value decreases, you're still responsible for paying the investment manager fees. Fees can reduce your overall nest egg.

One day in 1960 a guy named John Bogle came along and said, "What if we can create a mutual fund but without the fees of active management?" A whole new category of mutual funds called **index funds** came to fruition. Index funds changed the game because, unlike traditional mutual funds, they're passively managed. In other words, instead of paying a professional for active management, the fund follows a formula that eliminates the need for someone constantly buying and selling shares. It's a buy-and-hold strategy. The formula is designed to follow an index. Hence, that's why it's called index funds.

We will discuss more indexes later in chapter 9, but examples of indexes are S&P 500, Russell 2000, and Dow Jones Industrial Average. In other words, an index is a representative sample of the stock market to quickly measure stock market performance. Instead of looking up thousands of stocks individually, an index can be a measure to gauge overall performance.

John Bogle created the first index fund, which mirrored the S&P 500 index. The fund buys whatever stock is in the S&P 500, and the fees are much lower because you aren't paying fund managers to make decisions about which stocks to buy and sell. Instead of searching for a needle in the haystack, the fund buys the whole haystack.

After learning that the investing public had an appetite for such indexed funds, the race was on to make this style of investment more accessible to the investing public, since mutual funds often were expensive. ETFs are similar to index funds, and they were introduced roughly 15 years after index funds by Nathan Most. The only difference between index funds and ETFs is with index funds you can only buy and sell shares once a day. With ETF, you can buy and sell shares whenever the stock market is open.

Even though ETFs aren't stocks, you can buy and sell these baskets as though they are stocks. You can watch ETFs go up and down on a stock chart. ETFs offer 24/7 trading, which is different from a buy and hold strategy of an index fund. Remember, we're preparing for lifetime goals so the ability to trade often might not help with long-term success. ETFs can encourage more activity of buying and selling based on emotions. Many feel the strategy with index funds is simply to buy one, hold, and sell when you retire.

Mutual funds came first and offered the benefits of pooled investing. Then index funds came along as a special type of mutual fund, but with much lower fees because of their passive management. Lastly, ETFs arrived as an investment option, which trades like a stock. How they are bought and sold is the primary difference between ETFs and index funds. ETFs trade on an exchange just like stocks, and you buy or sell them through a broker. Index funds are bought directly by the fund manager. ETFs are bought and sold on an exchange, so you will pay a commission to your broker each time you make a trade, as you would any other stock.

Summary:

Investing in stocks, bonds, mutual funds, and ETFs are the most common types of investments. Stocks represent part ownership in a company with the potential for increased value. Bonds are loans from the company to investors, with interest paid at intervals and the principal repaid at the end of the term. Mutual funds are collections of money from many investors to invest in securities like stocks, bonds, and other assets. They are managed by investment professionals and offer diversification at a low cost. ETFs are similar to mutual funds but allow for 24/7 trading and have commission costs. They are bought and sold on an exchange, like stocks, and are bought directly with the fund manager. All of these investments offer different levels of risks and rewards, with stocks being the riskiest but potentially most profitable.

Action Steps:

1. Understand the basics of investing, such as stocks, bonds, mutual funds, and ETFs.

2. Learn about the parallels between playing golf and understanding the stock market.

3. Understand the different types of stocks, such as common and preferred stocks.

4. Learn about bonds and the federal bankruptcy laws, such as Chapters 7 and 11, that govern how US companies go out of business or attempt to recover from financial hardship.

5. Research mutual funds, index funds, and ETFs and determine which of these investments is best for your own retirement goals.

CHAPTER 6

Quick Start for Adults and Kids

Although this book is about different types of investments, not everyone is ready for investing. Before you start investing, it is best to pay off your debt and ensure you have an emergency savings fund. Looking around, it might seem like everyone is investing, but are you financially ready? Investing is an important part of your overall financial health, but many aren't ready for that step yet.

1. When you're setting up a financial plan, take time to think through the milestones you want to achieve and your priorities; otherwise, your money may be used in a way that doesn't align with your financial goals. For example, if you're buying a house within one year and decide to invest a large part of your savings into stocks, your money is no longer in alignment with your nearby purchase because of the risk of loss. If you need the money within a year, like for a down payment on a house, you'll need to invest differently than if you were to invest for retirement. **Before investing, take some time to list out your goals and rank them in order of importance, such**

as a child's college education, leaving an estate to your heirs, retirement, any sort of long-term considerations, etc. After you rank your goals, consider your risk tolerance. Ask yourself— at what point will a decline in your investments make you feel so uncomfortable that you'll want to make a change in how you're investing? Your risk tolerance will help inform the types of accounts that are best suited for you.

2. If you're still paying down high-interest credit card debt or personal loans, you may want to hold off investing. Low-interest rate debt can be OK such as mortgages, but a lot of high-interest rate debt and investing isn't a good combination. If you have high-interest rate debt, such as 20% on a credit card, it suggests you're looking to gain more than 20% by investing, which is considered speculative and risky.

3. Not having emergency savings before investing is a warning sign that you aren't ready. If you don't have emergency savings, your credit card remains the only option for basic expenses. Credit card debt should be avoided if possible. What will you do if your money is stuck in an investment account and you need to buy groceries for the week? You should always have three to six months of living expenses saved up on the side before investing.

4. While all the media coverage and rumors make it seem like many investors have earned high returns on their investments from crypto or single stocks, the reality is many also lost money as values plummeted over time. Doing your research will help you understand the types of risks involved in investing, which we've already addressed. Reading this book is a great first start to investing! You can also consider contacting a financial professional for assistance, such as one of the professionals at my company, Williams Financial

Group. Financial professionals are obligated to look out for your best interest; therefore, you won't be sold investments solely based on the highest commissions.

5. The best place to start investing is through an employer-sponsored retirement plan. Many offer some protection from the Employee Retirement Income Security Act (ERISA). ERISA protects retirement savings from mismanagement and abuse and holds those in charge of assets to be held to a high standard, such as acting in the best interests of the investors. Transparency and accountability are required, along with ensuring that participants have access to information about their plans. It is administered and enforced by three bodies: the Labor Department's Employee Benefits Security Administration, the Treasury Department's Internal Revenue Service, and the Pension Benefit Guaranty Corporation. In other words, you have a big brother trying to protect you from abuse. If your employer offers a 401(k), 403(b), 457(b), or pension, say yes! Before investing on your own, first, take advantage of what your employer is offering. In many ways, it teaches new investors some of the most proven investing methods: making small contributions regularly, focusing on the long term, and taking a hands-off approach. Most employer-sponsored retirement plans offer a limited selection of stock mutual funds, but not access to individual stocks.

After you have accomplished all five of those points listed above, you're ready for individual investing. There's no one-size-fits-all method for learning how to start investing. Below is a quick-start program for investing from A to F.

A. Decide how involved you want to be in investing in the stock market.

Figure out if you want to pick the stocks and securities or if you prefer a professional to do it for you. If you're picking your investments, there's research you must study, or if you're hiring a professional, you must know how to select an advisor, which is discussed in chapter 10.

B. Choose an investment account.

While it may seem easier to put all of your money in a savings account, that would force you to save far more money to reach the same goal. Choosing an investment account should be tuned to the goals you're pursuing when you invest. These are the major categories for investment account setup:

- Taxable Brokerage Accounts

- Employer Sponsor Retirement Accounts

- Individual Retirement Accounts

- Self-Employed Retirement Accounts

- Education Savings Accounts

- Health Savings Accounts.

Margin accounts for trading on margin and short-selling stocks will not be discussed, as these techniques are designed for advanced investors, as they are very risky. If you don't know what short selling is, you're in the right place.

Taxable Brokerage Accounts are available to anyone 18 years or older. If the investor is under 18, an adult will have to open a custodial account for them. For example, I opened a custodial account for my one-year-old son. Getting him early access! Taxable Brokerage Accounts are probably the type of account most people think of when investing. You deposit money into a brokerage account and then you use the funds to buy securities.

Employer Sponsor Retirement Accounts are offered as an incentive to recruit and retain top talent. They are tax-advantaged retirement accounts that many employers offer, such as 401(k), 403(b), and 457(b) plans. If your employer offers one of these plans, it must be available to all employees 21 years or older who have worked for the company for at least one year. The plan sponsor (usually the employer) chooses the investment options. It's generally limited to mutual funds, company stock, and annuities. Annuities are insurance contracts issued by financial institutions to pay out invested funds in fixed-income streams in the future.

Individual Retirement Accounts (IRA) are available in both traditional and Roth, just like Employer Sponsored plans. Roths have different tax advantages. Contributions to a Roth aren't tax-deferred. Instead, you make contributions with money that has already been taxed. Your investment earnings grow tax-free if you satisfy certain conditions. Traditional IRAs are tax-advantaged retirement investing accounts. Generally, you can deduct your contributions from your tax bill. Contributions grow tax-deferred until you withdraw them in retirement. Anyone with earned income can open an IRA.

Self Employed Retirement Accounts are for those who are business owners. Those who are self-employed can choose to open a solo 401(k), which can offer higher contribution limits than a self-employed IRA. With solo 401k(s) you can make contributions as both the employer and employee. They are only available to business owners with no employees besides spouses who work at least part-time.

Education Savings accounts make saving for tuition and educational expenses manageable. The two options for education savings are 529 plans and Coverdell education savings accounts (ESA). 529 Plans are investment accounts you can use for saving for a child's qualified education expenses, such as tuition, fees, and room and board at any college, trade school, or private school. Money is put into this account, pre-taxed, and as long as withdrawals are used to pay for qualified educational expenses, they aren't taxed. A Coverdell education savings account is similar to a 529 plan but with broader investment options. It can pay for private elementary, middle, and secondary school expenses in addition to tuition. The contribution limits are far less than a 529 plan. For example, in 2022, contribution limits for a Coverdell are $2,000 per year and a 529 is $15,000 per year with a five-year catch-up provision of $75,000 if you didn't make any contributions in five years.

Health Savings Account (HAS) is a tax-exempt account you can use to save specifically for medically related costs. To be eligible, you must be enrolled in a high-deductible health plan. Contributions to HSAs generally aren't subject to federal income tax, the earnings in the account grow tax-free, and the funds can be invested. Typically, the money goes unused for a long period, which could help with growth in the stock market. Some acceptable expenses under this plan would be programs to help stop smoking, purchase new eyeglasses and hearing aids, or modifications done to your home due to medical complications. The contribution limits are different for self-only than combined families, and the maximum amount limits change periodically. HSAs are attractive because there's no deadline to withdraw funds like in some retirement accounts such as a 401(k).

C. Learn the difference between investing in single stocks and funds

As I've mentioned before, funds let you purchase small pieces of many different stocks in a single transaction. When you invest in a fund, you also own a small share of each of those companies. Building a diversified portfolio out of many individual stocks is possible, but it takes lots of research and a large investment.

D. Set a budget for your investment

Share prices can range from a few dollars to a few thousand dollars, so plan well. Overall, a budget puts a person on a stronger financial footing for both the day-to-day and the long term. You can also learn about low-cost investments if you only have a small amount to invest. A tactic I used when setting up a budget is to make my goal very specific, such as "I want to have enough money to make a down payment on a summer home." After I make my goal specific, measurable, achievable, relevant, and time-based, my budget allocated for this investment will be in alignment.

E. Focus on lifetime investing

Stock markets will go up and down during the short run, however, over time, markets have appreciated. Stock markets have proven to be one of the best ways to grow long-term wealth no matter what's going on day to day. Many believe the best thing to do after you start investing is to not look at your statements often so that you can stomach the downside.

F. Manage your portfolio

Panicking over daily fluctuations might not be healthy for your portfolio, but periodic check-ins, such as annual or semiannually, is important to make sure your account is still in line with your investment goals. Review your portfolio with your advisor or make sure you understand everything on your investment statements. Don't worry if you don't understand statements because we will uncover this material in chapter 8.

Summary:

Before investing, it's essential to make sure you're financially ready. This includes having emergency savings and low-interest rate debt, avoiding high-interest rate debt, and listing out your goals and ranking them in order of importance. To start investing, consider taking advantage of employer-sponsored retirement plans such as 401(k), 403(b), 457, and pension plans, as they offer some protection from the Employee Retirement Income Security Act (ERISA). Other investment accounts, such as Taxable Brokerage Accounts, Individual Retirement Accounts, Self-Employed Retirement Accounts, Education Savings Accounts, and Health Savings Accounts, are also available. Set a budget for your investment and focus on lifetime investing, as stock markets have proven to be one of the best ways to grow long-term wealth. Finally, manage your portfolio with periodic check-ins and ensure you understand what's on your investment statements.

Action Steps:

1. Make sure you have emergency savings and don't have much debt before you start investing.

2. List out your goals and rank them in order of importance.

3. Avoid high-interest credit card debt, and if you have it, pay it off before investing.

4. Have three to six months of living expenses saved up before investing.

5. Take advantage of any employer-sponsored retirement plans first, such as 401(k), 403(b), or 457 plans.

CHAPTER 7
How to Read Stock Quotes

My first job out of college was as an investment banker for Merrill Lynch in the late '90s. I worked in the Mergers and Acquisition group, a prestigious group on Wall Street. I was a young man who people looked up to, so I had to look like I belonged. My suits were sharp, my briefcase was polished, I walked fast because I needed to look busy, and I always carried either the *Financial Times* or *Wall Street Journal*. The only problem was I didn't know how to read the market data and stock quotes because it was in a different format than how I learned it in school.

On my way to work, I would sit on the subway and stare at the finance section, pretending I understood what I was reading. But I had no clue! The same thing would happen when I watched CNBC in my office. What do all of these numbers, symbols, and colors mean that are scrolling across the bottom of my screen? So, let's learn how to allocate your focus and read the stock quotes on CNBC, Yahoo Finance, MarketWatch, Google Finance, Morningstar and more so you don't have to pretend as I did.

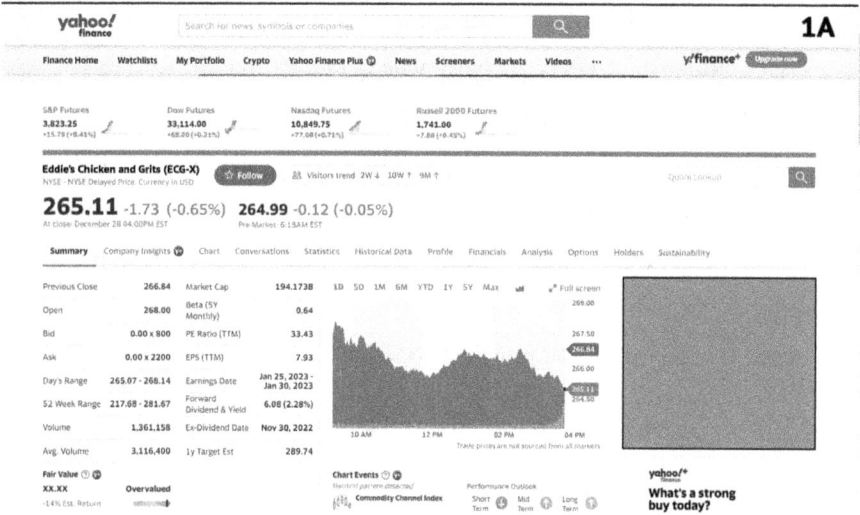

1A

Let's imagine my imaginary company Eddie's Chicken and Grits was a publicly traded company and listed on Yahoo Finance. I'll explain what you're seeing on the stock screener so you will have a basic understanding of how to read stock data. Please refer to chart 1A.

1. The name of my company, Eddie's Chicken and Grits, is listed on the top left corner along with the stock ticker symbol, which is the identifying letters of the stock.

2. The stock price is the bolded number 265.11 listed directly below the name of my company. One share of my company is worth $265.11. If the stock market is open, a fluctuating number will be next to it, which explains how much the stock either went up or went down during that trading day.

If the stock market is closed, the number will not fluctuate. My company went down $1.73 that day. The next number to the right shows the percentage increase or decrease for the last trading day. The company was down (-0.65%). Which is less than 1%. The final numbers on that row show the after-market trading. The stock will still be trading after the market closes and also pre-market, which is the next day before the market opens, but not nearly as much volume as normal market hours. My stock price has now dropped to $264.99 with trading after the market closed.

3. The previous close of the stock is the day prior to the market close of 4 pm. The previous close was $266.84 per share.

4. This morning the stock price opened at $268.00 per share. The previous day's close was $266.84. When the stock market opened at 9:30 am EST today, Eddie's Chicken and Grits started the day off at $268.00. It was a good morning.

5. Bid price is an intermediate concept we won't cover in this beginner's guide to investing, but it simply means the price people are willing to buy Eddie's Chicken and Grits per share.

6. Ask price is another intermediate concept we won't cover, but it means the price people are willing to sell Eddie's Chicken and Grits per share.

7. Days Range is the price fluctuation of the day. During today's trading day, Eddie's Chicken and Grit's share price fluctuated between $265.07 to $268.14.

8. The 52-Week Range shows you where the price of Eddie's Chicken and Grits has been in the past year. It has been as low as $217.68 and as high as $281.67. In other words, the current price of $265.11 is not near the lowest, and it's not near the highest point during the 52-week range.

9. Volume is very important. This shows how many shares of Eddie's Chicken and Grits have traded (shares bought and sold) this day. In other words, 1,361,158 shares have traded today. If you see a stock with a volume that is very low that means that you can get trapped in that stock because you wouldn't be able to sell it. A stock with a volume close to zero should be a red flag, because even if the stock price went up and you wanted to sell it, you probably couldn't get rid of it. If MY restaurant's volume is over a million shares and one share is $265.11, that means it's very liquid. Liquid simply means it's easy to buy a share of Eddie's Chicken and Grits and easy to sell a share since over a million shares trade hands each day.

10. The Avg. Volume is how many shares of this stock trade on average per day. The average volume is 3,116,400. Today's volume was less than the average, however, it's still very easy for you to sell your position and get out quickly because a lot of shares are trading each day.

11. Moving up to Market Cap, it reads 194.173B. The "B" after the number means billion, and "M" means million. Market Capitalization means the value of the company. The value of the company is how many shares in total of that company, multiplied by the price per share. So the value of Eddie's Chicken and Grits is over 194 billion dollars. Wow,

this would be my dream to own a company worth this much.

12. Beta is an intermediate terminology we won't cover in this beginner's guide to investing. Beta is a measurement of risk. The number 1 and below is normally considered lower risk, but ignore this number for now.

13. P/E Ratio is another intermediate term, which we'll cover in more detail in chapter 9. Price-to-earnings ratio indicates the dollar amount an investor can expect to invest in a company in order to receive $1 of that company's earnings. This is why the P/E is sometimes referred to as the price multiple because it shows how much investors are willing to pay per dollar of earnings. I know it can be confusing, but we will cover this concept thoroughly later.

14. EPS means earning per share. This is another intermediate term we will cover later. EPS refers to how much in net income the company makes divided by how many shares there are, that is why it's called "the earnings per share."

15. The Earnings Date is the expected date when the company will release its quarterly earnings. The earnings are expected to be released between January 25th and January 30th.

16. Forward Dividend & Yield means the dividend a company is paying. A dividend is the distribution of a company's earnings to its shareholders. Eddie's Chicken and Grits is paying a dividend yield of 2.28%. Not all companies pay a dividend. In other words, if you purchased $100 worth of Eddie's Chicken and Grits shock, you would receive a rate of 2.28%. If you brought $100 of this stock you would receive

$2.28 of dividends.

17. Ex-Dividend Date means the date required to have owned the stock before you can receive the dividend.

18. A one-year target estimate is something that is objective. It's not beginner-level material, but I believe you should do your own research and your own homework. Don't rely on other people's targets or estimates. This isn't concrete data like the other figures. This is simply an opinion.

Generally, the news will be displayed below the figure charts. This is important if there are large price fluctuations in the stock. You can read the news to learn why the stock drastically went up or down. If you're reading stock data online, you might want to watch out for the ads.

The charts and graphs are important as well.

1. 1D is the one-day chart. It shows the price movements of Eddie's Chicken and Grits for one day. The x-axes on the chart are showing the time of the day and the y-axes are showing the price.

2. You can switch the time frame to 5d (5 days), 1m (1 month), 6m (6 months), YTD (year-to-date), 1y (one year), 5y (5 years), max (how far the stock goes back from when it first became public) to see how the price fluctuates. You can see the prices drop at 12 pm. You might want to read the news to learn if anything triggered the drop in the stock price.

3. There will be features listed at the top header bar and the first tab is titled summary. We already reviewed everything in

the summary tab.

4. Company Outlook is locked because it's a paid service.

5. Charts were already reviewed.

6. Conversations are message boards with the public. It might be wise not to trust anyone from message boards.

7. Statistics is a more intermediate analysis that won't be covered in this beginner's guide to investing.

8. Historical Data is price closings from the past such as what the stock price was on a particular date or time frame.

9. The profile gives you more information about the company and the salaries of the top executives. This is an interesting page for many. It's essential to review who the top executives are and research them because leadership is crucial for company success. The profile also shows you the size of the company, the industry, the number of employees, the company website, and all of the basic information.

10. Financials is probably one of the most important segments. You can look at the income statement, balance sheet, and cash flow statement. When reviewing their income statement, it might be good to see if the company's total revenue is growing each year. Look at their total profits (net income) and look to see if it's growing every year or decreasing. This is a great way to look at financial health from a very high overview. You can do the same thing with the balance sheet. Are their assets growing, and are their

liabilities growing?

11. The analysis is opinionated, so it might be best to do your own analysis.

12. The option is an advanced topic that will not be covered in this beginner's guide to investing. Options are how investors can speculate on the future direction of a company, including profiting from company falls.

13. Holders are more intermediate material that a beginner will not need to know, but it explains who is holding the largest shares of the stock. People generally want what successful investors and investment companies are buying. It's good to know the large institutions that are also shareholders because it can be a signal of confidence for the public.

Those are the basics for how to read a stock quote on Yahoo Finance, but Google and many others are very similar.

Below is an imaginary ticker tape to help you understand the scroll at the bottom of financial news networks.

FUT - FV = IMPLIED OPENING PRICE

FUT (month) = future contract expiration date

FV = pre-market price

Energy futures price:

red = lower from last closing price

green = higher from last closing price

WTI = west texas intermediate crude
BRENT = crude from the north sea
NAT.GAS = natural gas

Change in Price

Stock or ETF symbol

Price Down

Corporation or ETF name

STOCK MARKET

WTI (May)	40.56
BRENT (Jun)	42.84
NAT. GAS (May)	1.929

207.65 ▼ 0.36

12.65 ▲ 0.38

8:00ᴀ EASTERN

previous closing price. Green indicates previous close was a price gain, red indicates a price drop.

FUT - FV = IMPLIED OPENING PRICE

FUT (month) = future contract expiration date

FV = pre-market price

s&p 500 fair futures

previous close. Red indicate lower, green indicates higher

s&p 500 fair value

s&p 500 previous close

STOCK MARKET

S&P FUT (Jun)	-4.75
S&P FV	-0.07
S&P CLOSE	2,082.78

0.21   Alcoa (AA) 9.93 ▼ 0.08   AAC Holdigs (AAC)   19.87 ▲ 0.34   Aaron

8:00ᴀ EASTERN

previous closing price. Green indicates previous close was a price gain, red indicates a price drop.

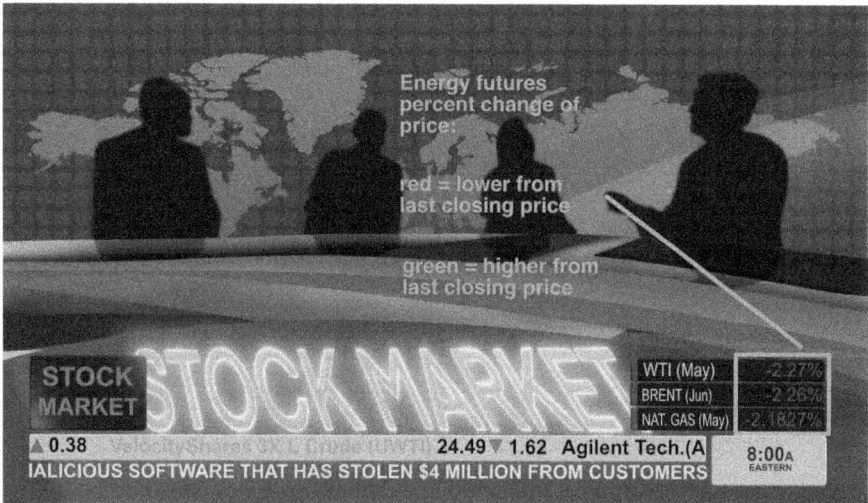

Summary:

This chapter provides an overview of how to read stock quotes, with a focus on Yahoo Finance. It explains the various pieces of data (e.g., stock price, bid price, ask price, volume, Market Cap, Beta, P/E Ratio, EPS, Earnings Date, Forward Dividend & Yield, Ex-Dividend Date, One-year target estimate, news, charts and graphs, Company Outlook, Conversations, Statistics, Historical Data, Profile, Financials, Analysis, Options, Holders) and how to interpret them. It also provides an example of a stock ticker tape from a financial news network and advice to do your own research and analysis.

Action Steps:

1. Familiarize yourself with the stock ticker symbols and the corresponding company names.

2. Observe the stock price and the amount it went up or down for the day.

3. Check the volume of trades for the stock to determine liquidity.

4. Read the news to understand why the stock price is fluctuating.

5. Analyze the income statement, balance sheet, and cash flow statement to assess the financial health of the company.

CHAPTER 8

Understanding Brokerage and Retirement Plan Statements

T oo many people don't open their brokerage or retirement plan statements that arrive in the mail before throwing them in the trash. I was one of those people. My reason for discarding my statements the moment they arrived in the mail was that I didn't need that negativity in my life. It was the same reason I didn't look at my bank balance when I withdrew cash from an ATM. I didn't want anything to affect my mood and make me feel miserable. My days were hard enough, and I needed every ounce of optimism just to get through them. If I didn't see my balances, I could still dream I was on my way to being a millionaire. I later realized this is a toxic approach to achieving financial freedom. By not looking at my statements, I didn't know my financial position and was unaware of the adjustments needed. **Financial success isn't accomplished with a set-it-and-forget-it strategy.**

You must know how your investments are performing, understand what you're paying in fees, when it's time to

rebalance your assets, etc. Not reviewing your statements can be compared to playing a basketball game and never knowing the score. There will be times when you need to raise the intensity, call a time-out to pause and slow the game down, hold the ball if you're winning to let time elapse, etc. How can you win? "An investment in knowledge pays the best interest" – Benjamin Franklin. Reviewing and updates are always needed. Your account statements keep the score of your investments and report all transactions during the statement period.

Some people might not open their statements because they don't understand them. They might glance at the statement and read the first page of whether money was made or lost and toss the statement in a drawer. These accounts may be the largest asset you will ever have, so it's important to understand. If you don't read or understand your statements, you might not spot mistakes or even outright fraud. Let's dive into it, so you can learn what you need to know, what's important, and what you should be looking out for with a brokerage or retirement statement such as a 401(k). The Department of Labor requires that your employer send 401(k) and brokerage statements at least quarterly, but there's no standardized format.

Statements From Employer Retirement Plans

Listed on the first page of the statement are common terms that can help you figure out how your investments are doing. Terms such as: beginning balance, contribution, withdrawals (if any), ending balance, and rate of return. The first four terms answer the questions of how much money you started with, how much money was put into the plan from you and your employer, if you took any out, and after those factors are considered, how much you will have remaining at the end of the quarter. The last common term is the rate of return, which ideally would be a positive percentage, but it might be negative in some quarters. We discussed the issue of investments being unpredictable, but over time, you should see enough positives to balance out the negatives. If you don't, that's a problem that should be addressed. Whoever issues your statement is required by law to put a phone number on the statement so you can call to ask questions about anything you don't understand.

Another term that should appear on your statement is the "vested balance." It's the portion of your balance that belongs to you. Your contributions are always yours for a 401(k), but sometimes your employer will set up their contributions to not vest immediately. We're addressing 401(k) plans because it's the most popular, but other retirement plans such as 403(b) and others are similar. For example, you might get an employer match on your 401(k) contributions as soon as you start working for a given company, but this contribution doesn't vest until you have worked there for five years. Employers do this to incentivize workers to stay at the company and protect the employer from losing money if workers leave.

Next, you'll want to look at the investment section of your statement, which will have a detailed list of where your money is currently invested. You'll see a pie chart breakdown of the different asset classes you're investing in and the percentage of your assets being invested in each. Keep a close eye on your investments to ensure your portfolio aligns with your risk tolerance level and goals.

Brokerage Account Statement

Your brokerage account statement is the official document for complete information pertaining to your account's value, holdings, and activity. Similar to employer retirement plans, account statements may look different from firm to firm but everyone has this information in common:

Account information – This shows the statement reporting period, your account number, your account type, your full name, and your address, and sometimes displays your account investment objective.

Account summary – Shows the beginning account value for the period, a summary of account activity including cash deposits, cash withdrawals, dividends and interest, fees charged, and closing account value for the period. This may also show a pie chart of the different asset classes and investments.

Income – This shows you the income and dividends earned by your investments for the statement period.

Fees – Brokerage fees are what a broker charges for various services, like subscriptions for premium research and investing data or additional trading platforms. Some even charge maintenance and inactivity fees. Some fees are baked into the mutual funds you've selected as an expense ratio, charged as a brokerage fee on your investment account, and added on as a stock trading commission when you buy or sell or levied by an advisor who is helping you sort through it all. It's important you know what you're paying.

Account activity – Displays the credits and debits of the securities transactions.

Margin – This is an advanced investor term that means your brokerage firm can lend you funds to pay for the securities being purchased.

Portfolio detail – Provides a complete inventory of the individual investments in your account. It includes the investment name, ticker symbol, share quantity, cost basis, current price, and current market value (quantity x price).

Disclosures and definitions – This provides legal and administrative explanations about fees, penalties, and the terms and codes used in your statement.

A major factor to account for with statements is your responsibility to check for inaccuracies or discrepancies. If you find any, you should contact your advisor immediately.

Below is a checklist for reviewing the accuracy of your statement.

1. Account number

2. Account type (individual brokerage account, joint brokerage account, margin, etc.)

3. Account name

4. Account investment objective (if provided)

5. Your contact information

6. Your brokerage firm, clearing firm, and financial advisor contact information. (Brokers are the conduit that enable customers to access the stock markets and place trades. Once that buy or sell button is hit and the trade is executed, the clearing firms handle the back office duties to ensure that

the trade and monies are settled and cleared.)

7. Know why your account increased or decreased in value from the previous reporting period.

8. Review account activity with special attention to fees, deposits and withdrawals, and transfers.

9. Review trade activity.

Understanding your 401(k) plan fees is a big deal. Not all 401(k) plans are created equally. Some have good low-cost investment options, and some are intertwined with insurance products and have high fees and high costs. All services have costs. To help you evaluate the cost of your plan, review the annual plan for your plan. Fees are paid for from your plan account and reduce your savings. Over time, this impact can add up. Many workers believe that 401(k) funds charge fewer fees than individual investments, but that is not always true. The US Department of Labor categorizes 401(k) fees as investment fees, plan administration fees, and individual service fees.

Investment fees are usually the largest portion of 401(k) fees, which includes the cost of investment management. Investment fees are generally charged as a percentage of assets. They can be broken down into expense ratios, and sales loads. Actively managed funds tend to have higher investment fees than passively managed funds like index funds.

Plan administration fees are fees for managing. Whether it's a bank or another financial institution, someone is managing your 401(k). Plan administration fees cover general management like record keeping, accounting, legal and trustee services. It also includes having access to customer service reps, educational seminars, and electronic access to plan information. The average plan administrator charges 1.3% to 1.5% annually (according to the nonpartisan Government Accountability Office.) That is $1,300 for every $100,000 invested, in order to participate in the 401(k).

Individual service fees are like additional administrative fees. They cover features you opted into, such as taking out a 401(k) loan, rolling over 401(k) investments into an IRA, or seeking financial advisory services. These are charged separately based on the participant using these features. Before you do anything other than basic buying and selling within your 401(k), inquire if the service is free or not.

Most 401(k) account holders will pay a wide range between .2%–5% in fees. These percentages might not seem like much but just a fraction of a percent could mean tens of thousands of dollars less in your total return.

To help investors make investment decisions, the Department of Labor introduced the fiduciary rule calling for 401(k) fees to be disclosed on statements. Still, many investment professionals claim 401(k) fees are hidden in plain sight. Administrators won't send you bills every quarter demonstrating how much you're paying for plan management and services. They also don't itemize fees on statements, instead, fees are shown in relation to the plan's reduced net returns. When you get your 401(k) statement, check for labels like "Total Asset Based Fees," "Total Operating Expenses As a %" or "Expense Ratios." While these technical terms may seem complex, it's possible to figure out what the numbers represent. To better grasp 401k terminology, please refer to your personal 401k statement.

Summary:

Many people avoid looking at their brokerage or retirement plan statements, as they may contain unpleasant information and evoke negative emotions. However, this toxic approach to achieving financial freedom is unhelpful and prevents you from being aware of adjustments that may need to be made. To achieve financial success, you must understand how your investments are performing, what you're paying in fees, and when it's time to rebalance your assets. Similarly, when it comes to a 401(k) plan, it's important to look at the first page of the statement to understand the beginning balance, contributions, withdrawals, ending balance, and rate of return. Furthermore, check the "vested balance," which is the portion of the balance that belongs to you, and the "investment" section, which displays a pie chart breakdown of the different asset classes. For a brokerage account statement, look out for account information, account summary, income, fees, account activity, margin, and portfolio detail. Lastly, it's your responsibility to check for inaccuracies or discrepancies, and if found, contact your advisor immediately.

Action Steps:

1. Open your brokerage or retirement plan statement when it arrives in the mail.

2. Understand the common terms on the first page of the statement, such as beginning balance, contribution, withdrawals, ending balance, and rate of return.

3. Review the statement's investment section for a detailed list of where your money is invested and the percentage of your assets being invested in each.

4. Look for labels such as "Total Asset Based Fees," "Total Operating Expenses As a %" or "Expense Ratios" on the statement to understand the fees you're paying.

5. Check for inaccuracies or discrepancies and contact your advisor if you find any.[4]

---

4   US Department of Labor .gov

CHAPTER 9
Which Stock Market

G rowing up, I had no idea there was more than one stock market. The only stock market I knew of was the New York Stock Exchange. The image I had in my mind was a madhouse of people screaming orders, loose paper on the floor, guys in suits, and complete chaos. This image isn't far off from reality—it's organized chaos.

A stock market is an umbrella term representing all of the stocks that trade in a particular country. However, it's often represented as an index or grouping of various stocks such as the S&P 500. The Standard and Poor's 500 (S&P 500) is an index tracking the stock performance of 500 large companies listed on stock exchanges in the United States. If this index tracks the 500 largest companies, why is "standard and poor" in its name? The history behind its name is in 1860, Henry Varnum Poor formed Poor's Publishing, which published an investor's guide to the railroad industry. In 1923, Standard Statistics Company began rating mortgage bonds and developed its first stock market index consisting of the stocks of 233 US companies computed weekly. In 1941, Poor's Publishing merged with Standard Statistics Company to form Standard & Poor's. On Monday, March 4, 1957, the index was expanded to its current 500 companies and was renamed the S&P 500 Stock Composite Index.

Many people don't know the difference between a stock market, a stock index, and a stock exchange, often confusing these terms with one another. There are many stock market indexes you might have heard of before, such as the S&P 500, Nasdaq, the VIX, Dow Jones, etc. Let's learn what a stock market index is and how it works. Stock market indexes are nothing more than a mathematical average that quickly tells you how the stock market is doing. There is no need to overcomplicate things. For example, if you and ten of your friends each weighed yourselves and you calculated the average weight of the entire group, that would be an index. As your weights changed, the index would change too. Anything that is a calculated average of many different components can be considered an index.

The S&P 500 is the most widely used stock market index and is the average of the 500 largest US companies all rolled up into one easy-to-read average price. Although there are well over 4,000 stocks in the US, the S&P 500 is a very accurate barometer of how the overall US stock market is doing because all of the largest and most influential companies are a part of this index. Generally, when you hear people say the market is up today, they are probably referring to the S&P 500. It's not because the S&P 500 is the stock market but because the index is a representative chuck of the market. The S&P 500 index sorts publicly traded companies into 11 sectors and 24 industry groups. The difference between a sector and an industry group as a sector is a broad classification and industry is a more narrow one. The industry refers to a specific group of similar types of companies and a sector describes a large segment of the economy.

The stock market is organized into two tiers. The highest tier is a sector, which is broken down into subcategories called industry groups. The 11 major sectors are used by most investors when breaking down the corporations and other issuers of securities such as stocks and bonds. Sectors and industry groups are often used interchangeably, but there's a distinction. For example, both Dollar Tree, a discount retail chain, and Tiffany & Company, a luxury jeweler, are included in the consumer discretionary sector but are sorted into different industries. They are two very different companies.

Overview of the S&P Sectors

1. Information Technology

The information technology (IT) sector consists of companies that develop or distribute technological items or services, including internet companies. Technology products include computers, microprocessors, and operating systems. Examples of companies in this sector include big names like Microsoft Corporation, Oracle Corp., and Mastercard Inc. This sector has seen a lot of change in recent years because of the rapid rise in technology-based companies.

2. HealthCare

Healthcare consists of medical supply companies, pharmaceutical companies, and scientific-based operations or services that aim to improve the human body or mind. Familiar names include Johnson & Johnson, a medical device and pharmaceutical company that owns Tylenol, and Abiomed, which manufactures medical implant devices. Cannabis companies are a new—but rapidly growing—part of the healthcare sector. Currently, the more well-known ones include Canopy Growth and Aurora Cannabis, with market caps of $23 billion and $12 billion, respectively.

3. Financials

The financial sector includes all companies involved in finance, investing, and the movement or storage of money. It includes banks, credit card issuers, credit unions, insurance companies, and mortgage real estate investment trusts (REITs)[5] Companies within this sector are usually relatively stable, as many are mature, well-established firms. Banks in this sector include Bank of America Corporation, JPMorgan Chase & Co., and Goldman Sachs. Other notable sector names include Berkshire Hathaway, American Express, and Aon PLC.

4. Consumer Discretionary

Discretionary consumer products are luxury items or services that aren't necessary for survival. The demand for these items depends on economic conditions and the wealth of individuals. Products include cars, jewelry, sporting goods, and electronic devices. Luxury experiences include trips, hotel stays, or dining in a posh restaurant. Most companies in this sector are widely recognized. Some examples include Starbucks, Best Buy, and Amazon.

5. Communication Services

The communication services sector consists of companies that keep people connected. This includes internet providers and phone plan providers. The more exciting part of the sector includes media, entertainment, and interactive media & services companies. Netflix Inc. and Walt Disney Co. are considered part of the communication services sector. Other companies within this sector include AT&T, CBS Corporation, and Facebook.

---

5   real estate investment trusts (REITs).

6. **Industrials**

Industrials include a wide range of companies, from airlines and railroad companies to military weapons manufacturers. Since the range of companies is so extensive, the sector has 14 different industries. Two of the largest industries are Aerospace & Defense and Construction & Engineering. The best-known names within this sector are Delta Air Lines and Southwest Airlines, FedEx Corporation, and Boeing Company.

7. **Consumer Staples**

Consumer staples companies provide all the necessities of life. This includes food and beverage companies, household product providers, and personal product providers. Consumer staple companies are well known since people see their products in stores regularly. For example, Procter & Gamble is a famous company in this sector, which produces bleach and laundry detergent under brand names like Dawn and Tide. Another example is Kroger, which is the largest supermarket chain in the US.

8. **Energy**

The energy sector consists of all companies that play a part in the oil, gas, and consumable fuels business. This includes companies that find, drill, and extract the commodity. Energy includes the companies that refine the material and companies that provide or manufacture the equipment used in the refinement process. Companies such as Exxon Mobil and Chevron extract and refine gas, while companies like Kinder Morgan transport fuel to gas stations.

9. **Utilities**

Utility companies provide or generate electricity, water, and gas to buildings and households. For example, Duke Energy generates and distributes electricity, and Southern Company provides gas and electricity. Many utility companies are developing more renewable energy sources.

10. **Real Estate**

As the name suggests, the newest addition to the S&P sectors includes Real Estate Investment Trusts (REITs), as well as realtors and other companies. The real estate sector makes up 2.9% of the S&P 500. Companies in the sector include American Tower Corporation, Boston Properties, and Equinix.

11. **Materials**

Companies within the materials sector provide the raw material needed for other sectors to function. This includes the mining companies that provide gold, zinc, and copper, along with forestry companies that provide wood. Companies not typically associated with materials but are in the sector include container and packaging companies such as the Intertape Polymer Group, a company that produces tape.

The 24 Industry groups are:

1. Automobiles and Components

2. Banks

3. Capital Goods

4. Commercial and Professional Services

5. Consumer Durables and Apparel

6. Consumer Services

7. Diversified Financials

8. Energy

9. Food, Beverage, and Tobacco

10. Food and Staples Retailing

11. Health Care Equipment and Services

12. Household and Personal Products

13. Insurance

14. Materials

15. Media and Entertainment

16. Pharmaceuticals, Biotechnology, and Life Sciences

17. Real Estate

18. Retailing

19. Semiconductors and Semiconductor Equipment

20. Software and Services

21. Technology Hardware and Equipment

22. Telecommunication Services

23. Transportation

24. Utilities

Other countries have their own stock market indexes. Japan has the Nikkei 225. Brazil has the Ibovespa. UK has the FTSE 100, etc. If you want to know how the country's economy is doing, you can review the stock market growth for that country. Stock market growth and decline often go hand and hand with economic growth and decline. Many people know that I decided to move to Italy to live and build my family before returning to the states. Before moving to Italy, I flipped to the back of *The Economist* magazine and there was a comprehensive list of all the countries and their stock market indexes. It gave me a good idea of how Italy's economy is doing. Knowing how the economy is doing in Italy was important because I was giving up my job in the US.

There are ten major indexes that all investors need to know about. Following these indexes will keep you informed about the economy and help you make smarter decisions about your money. **US corporations are very international and play a huge role in global markets.**

1. S&P 500 is the most followed stock market in the world. This index is the most important in my opinion. Before getting into the other indexes, let's dive deeper into the S&P 500.

2. Dow Jones is short for Dow Jones Industrial Average and is made up of the 30 largest companies in the US. These same 30 companies are already included in the S&P 500.

3. Nasdaq consists of over 3,000 stocks and has a heavy concentration of technology companies.

4. MSCI World Index covers all the major stocks across 23 developed countries. This is often used as metric for the

world economy as a whole.

5. MSCI Emerging Markets Index covers stock markets across 24 emerging market countries. Countries like Brazil, China, and India are all on this index.

6. S&P GSCI Commodity Index tracks commodities like oil, gold, silver, corn, cotton, wheat, cattle, etc.

7. Dow Jones Real Estate Index can be for a quick snapshot of how the real estate market is doing.

8. Dollar Index is another important index that tells you how strong the US dollar is, relative to other major currencies like the euro, pound, Japanese yen, Canadian dollar, etc.

9. VIX is also known as the fear index. The VIX gauges the level of fear present in the stock market by tracking the price levels of options. Options are complex financial instruments used as insurance against disaster. The VIX was very high during the financial crisis and the S&P 500 was very low. When the level of fear in the market rises, the VIX also rises.

10. Russell 2000 Index is the most widely used index of small-capitalization stocks, stocks with a relatively small market capitalization. It's widely considered the benchmark for smaller US stocks.

You might be wondering who calculates this stuff. Major financial data companies provide complimentary real-time calculation services of stock market indexes. For example, Dow Jones covers 30 large companies, which are subjectively picked by the editors of *The Wall Street Journal*. Over the years, companies have been changed to ensure the index stays current in its measure of the U.S. economy.

A stock exchange is a meeting place for buyers and sellers. Stock exchanges bring together the companies and current shareholders who want to sell stock and investors who want to buy stock from them.

A stock index is a gauge to read the whole market or sector of the market. In contrast, a stock exchange is a place where you buy and sell stocks, bonds, and other securities listed on various indexes. The most famous exchange is called the New York Stock Exchange (NYSE). The NYSE combines an electronic exchange with live people who help executive stock trades. The Nasdaq is the second largest exchange in the world, which is also located in New York, where traders buy and sell the stocks that make up the Nasdaq index. The Nasdaq stock market exchange is purely an electronic exchange, unlike the NYSE which also has live people. The Nasdaq is an exchange because it's a place where you buy and sell stocks, and the Nasdaq is also an index because it's a mathematical average that tells you how the stock market is doing for "technology stocks." When people ask, "How is the Nasdaq doing?", they aren't talking about the place, but instead, they are talking about the index. An index is simply a curated list of certain securities.

If the stock market is a giant jigsaw puzzle, the box would be the exchange, and you can think of an index as a magnifying glass. In the case of the Nasdaq, your magnifying glass allows you to take a closer look at a particular part of the puzzle, giving you a clearer picture of the finished product.

There are two commonly understood ways a company is considered public: (1) the company's securities trade on public markets, and (2) the company discloses certain business and financial information regularly to the public. Companies are subject to public reporting requirements if they: sell securities in a public offering such as an IPO (initial public offering), allow their investor base to reach a certain size that will trigger public reporting obligations, or if the company voluntarily registers with the SEC (Securities Exchange Commission).

If I wanted to have Eddie's Chicken and Grits IPO listed on an exchange, certain company qualifications must be met first. Companies generally go public because either they want to get out of debt or require financing not associated with the banking system. A significant reason why companies go public is to raise large amounts of money while spreading the risk of ownership to a huge group of shareholders. It's a major advantage to have your company's stock listed on the stock exchange. The factors that can qualify a company for an IPO are:

- A company has consistent and predictable revenue. A public market doesn't live for a company to "miss earnings" or have issues when predicting what they will be. Missing earnings means if a company reports earnings and their final numbers end up falling short of the consensus analyst estimate, they have missed their earnings number.

- The company needs to have the money to pay for the IPO process. It's very expensive to go public. The average cost of doing an IPO is around $750,000.

- The company still needs to have growth potential. The market will not want to invest in companies that have no growth opportunity. It will prefer businesses with consistent earnings but still have room for future growth.

- A company needs to be a major player in the industry.

As investors are searching for a niche of companies to buy into, they will assess them together for a while. If a company isn't performing as well or doesn't stand out against the competition, the investor will not be willing to pay much for it.

- The company needs to have a strong and experienced management team. Leadership quality is among the most significant considerations investors look into other than the financial aspect.

- Audited financials are required for all publicly traded companies.

- A company needs to have a low debt-to-equity ratio. It can make or break a successful IPO.

- Underwriters may require revenues of up to 20 million every year with one million profits.

Additional qualifications are needed before a company is listed on an exchange, but those are the most basic. Remember, there are over 4,000 public companies but only 500 are listed on the S&P, and only 30 are listed on the Dow Jones. Listing requirements comprise the various criteria and minimum standards established by stock exchanges, such as the NYSE, that companies must meet to list their shares for trading. A company will be allowed to list its shares for trading only if it meets initial and ongoing requirements. Companies that don't meet listing requirements on major exchanges may be able to offer their shares for trading over-the-counter market (OTC). OTC securities are securities not listed on a major exchange in the US and are instead traded via a broker-dealer network, usually because many are smaller companies and don't meet the requirements to be listed on a formal exchange.

There are three tiers to the OTC. You might have heard of one of them, which is pink sheets. It got its name because the original pink sheets listing the stocks were printed and distributed on pink pieces of paper. Most pink sheet stocks are considered penny stocks that trade for less than $5 per share. Pink sheet stocks are considered very risky due to the lack of regulatory oversight. Although pink sheet stocks are considered risky, some companies start off here and make it to major exchanges, such as Apple. Apple is by far the most popular penny stock that ever existed.

One critical step in investing involves learning how to read and figure out the key financial ratios. You have to know what they mean and what they can tell you, even if you get ratio figures from your advisor or a statement. For investors who are looking to invest beyond diversified mutual funds or ETFs, individual stocks can be a profitable option, but you need to know how to analyze their underlying businesses.

Reviewing a company's filings is a good place to start with the Securities and Exchange Commission (SEC). These filings will provide a great amount of information, including financial statements for the most recent year. From there, you can calculate financial ratios to aid your understanding of the business and where the stock price might be heading.

Just like stocks, mutual funds have their own ratios that investors need to look at to judge the investment worthiness of the fund. These ratios will help investors understand some of the key factors impacting their returns from mutual funds. As mentioned earlier, mutual funds offer the best of both worlds of investing in stocks and bonds directly. Mutual funds can diversify the investment into various equities and bonds, which reduces the risk of investing in single stocks. Let's have a look at key ratios for analyzing mutual funds and single stocks.

P/E ratio – P/E ratio stands for the price-to-earnings ratio indicating the dollar amount an investor can expect to invest in order to receive $1 of the company's earnings or "profit." It's often referred to as the price multiple because it shows how much investors are willing to pay per dollar of earnings. This is also important when analyzing stocks. It will provide a quick valuation of the mutual fund. Ideally, you always want this number to be as low as possible because mutual funds with a low P/E ratio would imply that it's cheap, and funds with a high PE ratio would imply the fund is currently expensive relative to the profit it makes. Since a mutual fund includes a number of stocks, the fund's P/E ratio is calculated by taking the weighted average P/E of all its underlying stocks in the proportion of their holding percentages. The calculation for the P/E ratio is the price per share/earnings per share. Earnings per share are explained later with the key stock ratios.

Let's determine the P/E ratio if Eddie's Chicken and Grits have a stock price of $60 per share and earnings per share of $3. Divide $60 by $3 to find out that Eddie's Chicken and Grits company has a price-to-earnings ratio of 20 times. This is telling us that the market is currently valuing the shares of Eddie's Chicken and Grits company at 20 times the amount of their yearly profit. So if you were to buy shares of Eddie's Chicken and Grits, you would be paying 20 times the amount that they generate in profit for the year. This ratio also implies that it would take 20 years at the current price and profit level for Eddie's Chicken and Grits to make enough money to pay back all the shareholders in full for their shares. The P/E ratio shows its strength when you use it to compare different companies or mutual funds within the same industry to get a better idea of how each company is being valued.

Expense ratio – The expense ratio is the percentage of total assets that a mutual fund charges an investor annually for managing their money. The expenses related to mutual funds fall into five categories, such as distribution charges, security transaction fees, management fees, investor transaction fees, and fund service charges. The expense ratio reduces the returns available to the investor. It might be best to look for funds that have lower expense ratios. According to Investopedia, which is the same company that owns Fox Corporation, "A good expense ratio, from the investor's viewpoint, is around 0.5% to 0.75% for an actively managed portfolio. An expense ratio greater than 1.5% is considered high." Expense ratios for mutual funds are typically higher than expense ratios for EFTs because EFTs are passively managed.

Alpha – Alpha denotes the excess return a fund gives you compared to a market benchmark or index. For example, if a mutual fund generates an annualized return of 10% as against an 8% given by the underlying benchmark, then the alpha is 2%. Hence, the higher the value of alpha, the more profitable it becomes for the investors.

Beta – Beta measures the risk or volatility associated with a fund in comparison to the market or benchmark. High Beta funds are more volatile than the benchmark. They tend to beat the benchmark when it goes up, but they also fall more than the benchmark when it comes down. This makes them riskier investments. You may pick high beta funds if your objective is to maximize your gains and are also prepared to bear huge losses. Less than 1 is a low beta, and greater than 1 is a higher beta.

Sharpe Ratio – Named after its creator Professor William Sharpe, this ratio enables one to judge the return from the fund in relation to the risk involved. In other words, the Sharpe ratio assesses the returns generated by a portfolio against per unit of risk undertaken. This ratio is useful if it's used only as a comparative tool. You can compare the Sharpe Ratio of a fund with that of its benchmark index. A higher Sharpe ratio will represent a higher return generated by a scheme per unit of risk taken.

In analyzing single stocks, the below ratios are important:

Earnings per share (EPS) – EPS is one of the most common ratios used in the financial world. This number tells you how much a company earns in profit for each outstanding share of stock. EPS is calculated by dividing a company's net income by the total number of shares outstanding.

P/E ratio – As explained in the key mutual fund ratios.

Return on Equity (ROE) – ROE is one of the most important ratios to understand or the Sreturn a company generates on its shareholders' capital. In one sense, it's a measure of how good a company is at turning its shareholders' money into more money. If you have two companies that each earned $1 million this year, but one company invested $10 million to generate those earnings while the other only needed $5 million, it'd be clear that the second company had a better business that year.

Debt to capital ratio – In addition to tracking a company's profitability, you'll also want to understand how the business is financed and whether it can support the levels of debt it has. One way to look at this is the debt-to-capital ratio, which adds short- and long-term debt, and divides it by the company's total capital. The higher the ratio is, the more a company is indebted. In general, debt-to-capital ratios above 40 percent warrant a closer look to ensure the company can handle the debt load.

Quick ratio – Also known as the acid test, the quick ratio measures whether a company can meet its short-term obligations with assets that can quickly be converted into cash. The ratio is useful for analyzing companies facing financial difficulties or during economic downturns when profits may be hard to come by. The ratio sums a company's cash, marketable securities, and accounts receivable, and divides it by its current liabilities. You can find all of these figures on the company's most recent balance sheet.

It's important to remember that none of these mutual funds and stock ratios in isolation are sufficient to select the right fund. 10 Investors need to use them in conjunction with each other to get reasonable results. Also, it's equally important to analyze these numbers concerning one's own financial goals 11 and risk appetite. Financial analysis using ratios is just one step in the process of investing in a company's stock. Be sure to also research management and read what they're saying about a business. Sometimes the things that can't be easily measured matter most for the future of a business.

I cannot end this chapter without discussing inflation. Inflation impacts every company and is a complex economics topic that is very relevant, with the inflation rate for the United States being 7.1% for the 12 months that ended in November 2022. Inflation is the rate at which the price of goods and services increases. As a result of inflation, the purchasing power of money decreases over time. Inflation affects the prices of everything around us. If someone earns a fixed income but inflation rises to 7% from 2%, their money will purchase 5% less than it did a year ago. This coupled with an investment loss on your money the same year can be significant. Understanding inflation is crucial to investing because inflation can reduce the value of investment returns. This erosion of real income is the single biggest cost of inflation. Imagine a family making $30,000 with no assets getting a 5% annual inflation rate. They see their expenses rise by 5% (losing $1,800 in buying power due to inflation) and have no way of making it up.

Inflation isn't always negative. Inflation is a net positive when it's moderate because it spurs wage growth and investment. High inflation is unsustainable and causes investors to hold onto money as opposed to spending. Low inflation, or worse, **deflation** (occurs when the inflation rate falls below 0%), is disastrous for an economy because products are no longer profitable to produce.

Currently, the economy is at an inflection with a high inflation point. The question is will we be able to get inflation back down? Will we be able to do it without causing a recession? How much more will the market continue coming down? All eyes are currently on the Fed (Federal Reserve) because it's their job to keep the economy healthy and keep inflation under 2%. The Fed job isn't easy. It's a delicate balancing act to keep inflation low and the economy growing well. It's challenging to do both at the same time.

In order to control inflation, the Fed has to raise interest rates, but raising interest rates slows the economy. It's kind of like trying to lose weight but also eating a lot of ice cream. It's hard to do both at the same time. This is the current debate right now. Will the Fed be able to lose weight and continue eating a lot of ice cream? In other words, get inflation down and keep the economy growing. If the Fed cannot pull this off, we will get something called Stagflation. Stagflation is high inflation and a stagnating economy. Just think of higher food and gas prices but less income and fewer jobs. It's a bad combination.

Stagflation can also be bad for the stock and bond markets. In the 1970s, when there was stagflation, the stock market fell a total of 60% from the high before it started to turn around. Despite stock prices suffering this year, many believed as long as the Fed kept raising interest rates at a good pace, we would probably get back on track with inflation, and the economy would continue to grow. Then Russia invaded Ukraine. Many believe these repercussions go way beyond the borders of Russia and Ukraine because Russia produces 10% of the world's oil. Russia and Ukraine together are basically like the world breadbasket. Together they export more than 25% of the world's wheat. The countries are also key suppliers of many other important commodities like corn, barley, and metals used to produce cars and semiconductors.

Perhaps given this huge external shock factor, this is why inflation went from being a code yellow issue to a code red issue. Who knows? Now it's no longer an easy fix to raise interest rates little by little so that inflation will go away. Now the Fed is stuck between a rock and a hard place because in order to stop inflation, it would appear that we need aggressively higher interest rates, which could cause a recession. But not being aggressive about raising rates could mean that inflation would sparrow out of control. So, it's hard to control inflation while not causing a recession. As stated, it's like trying to lose weight while eating ice cream. It's hard to do both. Some people feel that inflation will go away on its own and that it's only temporary. No one really knows what caused it, or when it will go away. There are monthly inflation data releases that you can track on the Bureau of Labor Statistics website www.bls.gov.

Remember, a diversified portfolio is beneficial. If the US goes into a recession, that doesn't mean Asia, Europe, Latin America, and the rest of the world will be in a recession. In this case, international diversification is advantageous. Emerging Markets are markets that aren't as much linked to what is going on in the US economy and include countries such as India, China, Brazil, etc. Developed Markets are Canada, Australia, Japan, and Europe. So, diversity might help with inflationary environments. Some assets have benefited from inflationary or recessionary environments in the past, such as inflation-protected bonds, real estate, commodities, and gold. Again, no one knows how the stock market will react to inflation, but as a general rule, it's good to be diversified instead of having all of your eggs in one basket.

Summary:

The stock market is an umbrella term representing all of the stocks that trade in a particular country, represented as an index or grouping of various stocks, such as the S&P 500. The S&P 500 is an index tracking the stock performance of 500 large companies listed on stock exchanges in the United States. It's made up of 11 sectors and 24 industry groups and is the most widely used stock market index. Other countries have their own stock market indexes, such as Japan's Nikkei 225, Brazil's Ibovespa, and the UK's FTSE 100. The New York Stock Exchange and Nasdaq are the two largest stock exchanges in the US. Companies must meet certain qualifications to be listed on an exchange, such as having consistent and predictable revenue, paying for the process of IPO, having growth potential, being a major player in the industry, having a strong and experienced management team, having audited financials, and having a low debt to equity ratio.

There are various requirements for a company to be listed on a stock exchange, with the NYSE having the most stringent. Companies not meeting the listing requirements can still offer their shares for trading via the over-the-market (OTC), such as pink sheets. Investors must understand the key financial ratios when investing in stocks and mutual funds, such as the P/E ratio, expense ratio, alpha, beta, Sharpe ratio, earnings per share, return on equity, debt to capital ratio, quick ratio, and inflation rate. It's important to analyze these ratios in relation to one's financial goals and risk appetite and to be diversified to manage the effects of inflation.

Action Steps:

1. Research management and read what they're saying about a business to better understand a company's stock.[6]

2. Consider diversifying a portfolio to include inflation-protected bonds, real estate, commodities, and gold to help mitigate the effects of inflation.[7]

3. Analyze financials to determine if a company meets the listing requirements of a major exchange or qualifies to be traded over-the-counter market (OTC).[8]

4. Research management and read what they're saying about a business to get a better[9] understanding of a company's stock.[10]

5. Consider diversifying[11] a portfolio to include[12] inflation-protected bonds, real estate, commodities, and gold to help mitigate the effects of inflation.[13]

6   Fidelity Investments Research

7   The S&P Sectors by CFI Team

8   https://corporatefinanceinstitute.com/resources/knowledge/finance/reit-real-estate-investment-trust/

9   An Introduction to US Stock Market Indexes - Investopedia

10   Upcounsel by William Cate

11   https://mutualfund.adityabirlacapital.com/blog/biases-you-should-never-have-while-picking-a-mutual-fund

12   https://mutualfund.adityabirlacapital.com/blog/aiming-for-financial-freedom-start-with-your-goals

13   Ukraine Invasion Threatens Global Wheat Supply, The New York Times

CHAPTER 10

I Want to Invest, Who Do I Call?

Recently, I was introduced to a new financial advisor in my area. I asked all the right questions but did not feel comfortable with the answers. I was becoming concerned. It turned out that the financial advisor wasn't registered with Financial Industry Regulatory Authority (FINRA) or the SEC. After conducting additional homework, I learned that the financial advisor was an insurance agent selling only annuities and life insurance. I was confused because he walked the walk and talked the talk, and even introduced himself as a financial advisor, which can be unclear to the uneducated client.

Can the agent call himself a financial advisor? Can you explain the difference between a financial advisor, banker, or insurance agent? These were the questions I received from one of my clients. It's a popular question because people are often confused about the differences. We'll highlight the differences in this chapter. Now that we understand the power of the stock market, who do we trust as our guide? How do you find conflict-free advice? How do we know the advice we're getting doesn't benefit the person on the other side of the desk? Sometimes going back to your professional to help you save on fees is like going to your pharmacist to help you get off meds.

Anyone can call themselves an advisor, but to be a registered financial advisor, one must complete certain training requirements, pass qualifying exams, register with the state, and go through background checks. Anytime I see an insurance agent who doesn't have any securities licenses calling themselves a financial advisor, that is when things seem to be fishy. Imagine you're in the market for a used car, and you want to choose between all the different makes and models. You go to a dealership that claims they can offer everything. Then once you get there, you realize you can only purchase a Ford, specifically a Ford pickup truck. Unfortunately, that's all they have to offer. Now think of an advisor who says they can offer you comprehensive financial planning, but at the end of the day, the only thing they can offer you is life insurance. Life insurance isn't a bad thing, but it's not right for every single person during every situation.

If someone is looking for comprehensive financial planning, consider going to someone who can offer you annuities, life insurance, investments, stocks, mutual funds, etc. If you find yourself in a similar situation with a financial advisor who appears skeptical, ask them who are they registered with, who are they licensed through, and how can you research them through brokercheck.com. Brokercheck. com is an online free tool from FINRA that can help you research the professional backgrounds of brokers and brokerage firms, as well as investment adviser firms and registered advisers. It allows you to check the licenses and the disciplinary record to make sure the adviser hasn't had any run-ins with regulators or the law.

In the financial services industry, there's no shortage of people calling themselves financial advisors wanting to give you financial advice.

Stockbrokers, CPAs, insurance agents, investment advisors, financial planners, and even some attorneys are calling themselves financial advisors. But how many of these individuals are genuinely interested in providing you with financial advice? Which ones would you rather sell your products and services to? Which ones are looking out for your best interests as opposed to their own? Although the answers to those questions can have a critical impact on your financial success and your family's financial security, most individuals have no idea what differentiates one financial advisor from another. So let's find out.

Insurance agents, financial advisors, and bankers share some of their job duties, but they also have many unique job responsibilities specific to their job professionally. The financial advisory process may sometimes be complex. Technical jargon is used and various people in the industry all claim to be able to advise the average person on the street.

In America, there's no shortage of finance professionals whose job is to advise people on personal finance matters.

The three most common finance professionals are 1) Insurance Agents, 2) Financial Advisors, and 3) Personal Bankers.

Before we go into the differences, let's first understand what each group does.

Insurance Agents:

An insurance agent represents one or more insurance companies and sells their policies for a commission. They can work full-time in insurance sales for an agency or as independent contractors. Their job is to represent the insurance company in the transaction while also helping customers find the right coverage. Insurance agents are generally appointed representatives of life insurance companies. They may choose to specialize in a certain area, such as property and casualty insurance (P&C), which protects a business against lawsuits and property losses. They will advise you on your insurance or investment needs based on the products their insurance company provides. Also known in the industry as a tied agent, they have a responsibility to act in the best interest of the insurance company they represent.

They may also be allowed to advise you on products from other financial institutions if the insurance company they represent has partnerships with other insurance companies. For example, XYZ agents who represent XYZ will advise you on products mainly from XYZ. ABC agents will advise you on products mainly from ABC. HIJ agents will advise you on products mainly from HIJ.

Financial Advisor:

A financial advisor is a professional who provides financial services to clients based on their financial situation. Financial advisors must complete specific training and be registered with a regulatory body in order to provide advice. Many financial advisors work for larger firms. An independent financial advisor is someone who works on their own to provide financial advice to clients. Appointed representatives from Independent Financial Advisors (IFA) are financial advisors who advise you on products from the IFA firms they represent. IFA firms are called independent because they can offer you products from different companies. Their recommendations are to be independent, and they aren't allowed to be influenced by companies.

For example, QRS-appointed representatives can advise on products based on QRS partnerships that are in place.

Personal Bankers:

Personal bankers are responsible for providing customer service and support to clients of a financial institution. It involves working one-on-one with clients, explaining financial products, and assessing their needs. Personal bankers are appointed representatives of a bank. They can advise you on products offered by their bank as well as life insurance products from companies their bank has agreed to distribute from. For example, a personal banker from DEF will be able to offer you products from DEF and Eddieslife since Eddieslife has an existing partnership with DEF.

What Are the Key Differences in Their Roles

On the surface, all three types of appointed representatives may appear to have similar job scope, which is to advise on insurance and investment products offered by their company or products from other financial institutions that their company has agreed to distribute. However, there are notable key differences people should know of.

1. An insurance agent will usually offer life Insurance products offered by the company they represent

Generally speaking, the logic is simple. If we see an insurance agent from Yourlife Company, we would expect him or her to offer us products from Yourlife Company. The same applies to tied agents of other insurance companies. Consumers might want to ask questions whenever an insurance agent tries passing off their company's products as superior to others by comparing them favorably to other similar insurance products in the market.

Strictly speaking, some agents may not be allowed to advise on other companies' products. If they try to pass off their products as superior to others, remember they're in a conflict-of-interest situation. It's important to research the product, company, and agent.

Financial advisors should be unprejudiced in a broader product mix such as stocks, bonds, mutual funds, etc.

They should advise you on products in an unbiased way. Financial advisors offer impartial advice on financial matters tailored to meet your needs and objectives. However, always bear in mind that there are limitations. Financial advisors, regardless of how unbiased they may be (or claim to be), may have differing levels of knowledge in various products. Differing levels of knowledge can make a financial advisor less prejudiced because the advice is based on their knowledge. Even if you're working through representatives from IFA, make an effort to understand their comparison and on what basis they are making their recommendations.

Personal Bankers are paid a salary.

Unlike most agents or financial advisors who are paid solely through commissions, personal bankers are employees of the banks they represent. They earn a basic salary and commission for the work they do. However, just because a person receives a basic salary doesn't instantly make them "better" to turn to. In return for the salary they are paid, most personal bankers are required to meet sales targets. They do so mainly in two ways. Firstly, they service walk-in customers. These are customers who are sometimes referred to them by the front-line bank tellers. Personal bankers will advise these customers on products offered by the bank and its affiliates. These may be CDs, mortgages, insurance products, etc., that the bank distributes. Secondly, personal bankers also spend their time (usually after office hours) calling and soliciting more sales. These could be based on existing bank customers as well as new leads that a personal banker may generate on their own through roadshows or other events they attend. At the end of the day, personal bankers are employees of the banks they work for and are expected to meet the Key Performance Indicators (KPIs) set for them.

Which Is Better and Who Should You Choose?

An appointed representative, be it an insurance agent, financial advisor, or personal banker, is ultimately looking to advise you on products that they distribute. This isn't necessarily a bad thing because the professional might be very knowledgeable with their product suite. The problem exists when the professionals don't offer full disclosure of the product and the type of advice they can legally provide. If someone wanted to purchase a Ferrari, they wouldn't go to a Ford pickup truck dealer if they knew it was a Ford dealership.

The financial services industry has many caring people of the highest integrity who genuinely want to do what's in the best interest of their clients. Unfortunately, many are operating in a "closed-circuit" environment in which the tools at their disposal are pre-engineered to be in the best interests of the "house." The system is designed to reward them for selling, not for providing conflict-free advice. The product they sell you doesn't necessarily have to be the best available, or even in your best interest. By legal definition, all they have to do is provide you with a product that is "suitable." What kind of standard is "suitable?" Do you fly the airline with a "suitable" safety record? Or better yet, "Let's go to lunch here; I hear the food is suitable." A good place to start for receiving conflict-free advice is with a fiduciary. We addressed how advisors will generally only offer you advice based on the products they can distribute, but that isn't always true.

Fiduciary is a legal standard of advisors who get paid for financial advice and, by law, must remove any potential conflicts of interest (or at a minimum they must disclose them) and put the client's needs above their own. For example, if a fiduciary financial advisor tells a client to buy Eddie's Chicken and Grits stock and later that day also purchases the stock for himself at a better price, he must give the client his stock at the lower price trade. Imagine having investment advice where you knew that the law protected you from your advisor steering you in a specific direction or to a specific product to make more money off of you. The fee you pay a fiduciary for advice may be tax deductible, depending on your tax bracket. Most people don't know if their advisor is a fiduciary or not, but everyone believes an advisor should have their client's best interest at heart.

Aligning yourself with a fiduciary can be a good thing, but this doesn't necessarily mean that the professional you select will provide good or even fairly priced advice. As with any industry, not all professionals have equal skills or experience. Sometimes the added cost of a fiduciary may only be justifiable if they are adding value, such as tax-efficient management, retirement income planning, and greater access to alternative investments beyond index funds.

Choosing a financial advisor can be an overwhelming process due to the standards of care each financial professional must provide. Financial designations are credentials that financial industry professionals use that indicate a degree of education and specialization on the part of the individual. Professional designations provide a standardized way for people to convey their expertise and are represented by letters after a name, such as CFP (Certified Financial Planner), CPA (Certified Public Account), and CFA (Chartered Financial Analyst). These three designations are the most popular among the hundreds of others because they require extensive knowledge, continued education, and adherence to strict codes of ethics. It's important to note that not all letter combinations require the same degree of knowledge and training.

Finding an advisor isn't as simple as going with the person your friend suggested or the insurance broker assigned to you. You need to actively search for someone who will work in your best interest, which takes some time. **If your selection process is well-researched, you'll have a better chance to gain better advice, a higher probability to save money, and potentially earn more while achieving your financial goals.** That could be worth the extra legwork in helping you find an advisor you can work with for a lifetime.

Summary:

When considering who to trust with financial advice, it's imperative to understand the different roles of insurance agents, financial advisors, and personal bankers. Insurance agents represent one or more insurance companies and sell their policies while financial advisors provide impartial advice on financial matters tailored to the client's needs and objectives. Personal bankers are employees of the banks they represent and are paid a salary and earn a commission when they meet sales targets. When an insurance agent tries to pass off their company's products as superior, make sure you ask questions and do the extra legwork of researching the product, company, and agent when considering who to turn to. Financial designations such as CFP, CPA, and CFA are credentials used to indicate a degree of education and specialization. When selecting an advisor, it's important to research and find someone who works in the best interest of the client.

Action Steps:

1. Research the qualifications and credentials of any potential financial advisors you're considering.

2. Ask the financial advisor who they are registered and licensed through, and research them on Brokercheck.com.

3. Ask questions and make sure to understand the differences between insurance agents, financial advisors, and personal bankers.

4. Look for a fiduciary financial advisor who is legally obligated to put your interests first.

5. Investigate the designations and credentials of any potential financial advisors.

CHAPTER 11

Slang Expressions That Make Investing Fun

I trade size all day every day, so we're going to hunt elephants and go long on that because I see the upside everywhere. Treat me subject because I'm junked up on Venezuelan for 10 years, and it's not held, so put it on the tape if you're not stopped out. Wall Streeters, like any other group of people, have their own language based on what they do and see every day. Their language is based on money. Wall Street recognizes a different language and culture that permeates the business. Each area of research, sales, trading, investment banking, and money management has its jargon that can be interchangeable

Let's learn the basics of investing slang. It's hard to be in a world where you don't understand the language. When I began my first job out of college working on Wall Street, I had a lot to learn. I was unfamiliar with a lot of the jargon and felt left out of other's group conversations. I remembered forcing myself into conversations and not knowing how to respond. There was one conversation I can never forget. I worked for Merrill Lynch in the World Trade Center in the early 2000s, and every day after work, many of the workers headed down to a restaurant called Moran's for happy hour.

I went there for a drink one day after work and noticed a woman across the bar who I wanted to meet. I approached her immediately and introduced myself. I can't remember her name because we only chatted for five minutes, and I never saw her again, but I still remember my response to the question she asked me over 20 years ago. I was trying so hard to be cool with my dark suit, polished shoes, leather briefcase, and Merrill Lynch investment banking business card easily accessible for disbursement in the left inside pocket of my suit jacket. The conversation went like this: "Hello, I'm Eddie. Saw you from across the bar and wanted to come over to meet you. Would you mind if I joined you for a drink?" She said, "Sure," which I was thrown off guard because I had never asked a woman for a drink outside of a college bar, so I was expecting her to tell me she was waiting for her kids or husband or something.

After I sat next to her, she asked me if I worked for Merrill as well, and I casually said, "Yep," as though I had been working there for years. I didn't want her to know it was my first week working a professional job out of school. After I responded, she asked about my previous job and revealed she had come from the buy-side. When she said she came from the buy-side, I had no idea what she was talking about nor what side I was on. I immediately felt embarrassed because my cover was blown. I tried coming off as a polished executive, but I didn't know the simplest question. I immediately picked up my phone and pretended someone was calling me, stood up, and said, "I have to return to my office for a work emergency." I handed her my business card and walked out quickly.

It was the weirdest interaction. That one experience gave me a lot of embarrassment. The next day I ran into my boss's office and asked him to explain the terminologies. The woman at the bar never called me, and I never saw her again. If the woman from Moran's is reading this book, please excuse me for leaving so rudely, but I didn't know how to respond and I felt exposed. I didn't want to say something dumb like I'm on the west side.

I worked in the mergers and acquisitions group, which I now know is referred to the sell-side. **The buy-side refers to firms that purchase securities and includes investment managers, pension funds, and hedge funds. The sell-side refers to firms that issue, sell, or trade securities, and includes investment banks, advisory firms, and corporations.**

The most common stock market slang words include "bear market" (a market in which prices are falling), "bull market" (a market in which prices are rising), and "blue chip" (established, safe, and highly valued companies). Fancy financial jargon has long made the stock market feel inaccessible to many people, but I've included common slang terms below to help minimize those barriers.

Of course, I don't expect anyone to memorize all of these terms, but I've found that memorizing a few and using them in your conversation makes investing fun because you're socializing your learning. Investing can be fun and enjoyable to talk about, not to mention that knowing the lingo is a handy tool for getting an insider's perspective. When speaking this language, it's a way of signaling "we belong to this community."

All the Boats Rise	When the tide comes in, all the boats rise. When the stock market quickly rises, most stocks tend to increase in value due to over-optimism. The opposite is, *When the tide goes out, all the boats sink*, which is due to over-pessimism.
ARG	Aggressive revenue growth.
Bear Hug	When a company offers to buy another company at a significant premium. A high offer price intends to entice shareholders of the target company to vote in favor of a merger and against its management. Usually considered a hostile takeover offer.
Bearish	To believe the market will go down.
Black Monday	The day the stock market crashed on October 19, 1987.
Black Friday	The Friday after Thanksgiving, a very popular shopping day for retailers. *In the black* means to be profitable. A very recent and annoying cliché, as it conjures up memories of 1987 and 1929.
Black Tuesday	The day the stock market crashed on October 29, 1929.
Bottom Fishing	After a large sell-off or drop in the market, a slang term for picking oversold stocks.
Bullish	To believe the market will go up.

Buy & Hold	A foolish method of investing. When you buy a stock and forget about it indefinitely. Jim Cramer's term *Buy & Homework*, or to evaluate your portfolio periodically, is more practical.
Castles in the Sky	When stock prices are extremely overvalued and not justifiable by future increases in earnings. 1987 and 1999 are examples, just before large market drops.
Chasing Returns	(1) Taking on more risk to gain a higher return. Banks buying more SIVs (risky debt) to gain higher returns greatly contributed to the liquidity crisis of 2007–09, as many of the SIV funds became insolvent. (2) When a group of stocks or the entire market has experienced a high return and investors invest more into this group just for that reason. Often *P/E Inflation* occurs as a result, when such stocks rise in price while their earnings don't go up quite as much. [P/E = price divided by earnings.]
Closing Bell	When trading stops on the New York Stock Exchange and Nasdaq each day, a bell is rung to signal the event.
Crash	A large sell-off (-10% or more) in the stock market in a single day.
Crowding Out	When the Federal Government incurs massive budget deficits, it must borrow tremendous sums of money. This effectively "crowds out" private businesses from borrowing in the capital markets as there's less money available for loans.

Dead Cat Bounce	After a stock (or even the entire market) has dropped substantially, there's often a moderate bounce to the upside. This bounce may be caused by value investors believing the stock had become undervalued at this beaten-down price, or by short sellers covering their positions as shorting was compounding on the way down.
Dovish	When the Federal Reserve Governors imply that interest rates may be going down soon. The opposite of *hawkish*.
Field Bet	Buying a group of stocks in the same industry, most often when a group is unprofitable and oversold. The theory is that some companies may go bankrupt, but one or more may survive and incur large gains in the stock price.
Flash Crash	A crash in stock prices caused by computerized automated selling that can result in a 5% to 10% drop in the market within an hour or two. A precursor to such an event is often extremely negative market futures just before opening. Volatility is extreme during flash crashes due to automated buying and selling. Large trading errors have also caused flash crashes, like erroneously selling 1,000,000 shares of a stock, instead of $1,000,000's worth.
Gentlemen Prefer Bonds	An obsolete saying used in a long-term bear market for stocks. Bonds tend to outperform stocks during recessions.

Hawkish	When the Federal Reserve Governors imply that interest rates may be going up soon. The opposite of *dovish*.
Joe Granville Wednesday	The Dow Jones Industrial Average hit 1,000 on Tuesday, January 6, 1981, after not reaching 1,000 since January 26, 1973. On Wednesday, January 7, 1981, Joe Granville announced in his investment newsletter to "Sell Everything!" The Dow dropped by more than 7% in the next six weeks, which made him quite famous. The Dow kept falling until August 1982.
Limit Down	Price controls on futures contracts, which halt trading after a large drop.
Merger Monday	Mergers, or companies buying other companies, often consummate a deal over a weekend and then publicly announce it on a Monday.
Misery Index	The unemployment rate and the inflation rate added together. The term was made famous by President Jimmy Carter during his 1976 presidential campaign.
Nifty Fifty	A group of 50 large cap overvalued stocks that greatly influenced the market in the 1960s.
Opening Bell	When trading starts on the New York Stock Exchange and Nasdaq each day, a bell is rung to signal the event.

Painting the Tape	When a group of investors illegally move a stock by trading it all at the same time. This happens every day, just watch the tape of most active light volume stocks, but don't get sucked in. Day trader newsletter emails can cause such moves.
Quadruple Witching Hour	The final hour of trading on a Friday when stock index futures, single stock futures, stock index options, and stock options all expire. This happens on the third Friday in March, June, September, and December. This used to be called the *Triple Witching Hour*.
Random Walk	A 1970s author created a portfolio of stocks by throwing darts randomly at a newspaper stock price table. The dart portfolio outperformed the collective results of a sideways market.
Rubber Band Effect	After a large sell-off in the market, there is a tendency for the market to bounce back right away. It's caused by computerized trading programs. It's also known as a V rally due to how it appears on a chart.
Sell in May and Go Away	The market is often seasonal, rising in late winter at times. The market can run out of steam in May, with stock prices falling, causing the *Summer Doldrums*.
Shimming	Stealing a few pennies from trades by specialists or market makers. See *Trading Ahead*.

Stagflation	A state of the economy when Unemployment is high and Inflation is high. Quite often, stagflation is caused by massive deficit spending by the Federal Government. This deficit spending reduces private sector output with higher inflation.
Summer Doldrums	Stocks tend to remain flat or drop during the summer. Many people are on vacation, with trading volume usually dropping also.
Trading Ahead	Unethical and illegal trading by specialists or market makers. A specialist may buy a stock for themselves from John Q. Public even though a better price is available from another seller. The specialist can view bids and ask prices and then manually mismatch them, or *see ahead* to a less favorable price. It happens all the time in this editor's experience, by observing how long it takes for a stop order to execute after the stop price was reached. This practice is a form of *shimming*.

Trading Imbalance	A situation where a large block of stock is put up for sale, but not enough buyers are available for purchase, and a market maker is unable to buy the imbalance. Lightly traded and tightly held stocks are considered temporarily illiquid during such imbalances. On occasion, a trading halt is put into place until enough buyers are available to purchase the deficit. On rare occasions, a handful of buyers can buy the stock at a huge discount if the stock was not halted during the imbalance. On the New York Stock Exchange, large stocks usually have a "delayed open" for such imbalances, as a trading specialist will fill the order by lining up buyers for the block, and then open trading for the stock for the day.
Triple Witching Hour	The final hour of trading on a Friday when stock index futures, stock index options, and stock options all expire. This happens on the third Friday in March, June, September, and December. See *Quadruple Witching Hour*.
Unicorn	A privately held company that had quickly reached one billion dollars in revenue and is now considering going public. Such companies appear to be "mythical" like a unicorn due to their swift growth, and investment banks may actually hesitate to bring them public. Fast-growing large companies awaiting favorable market conditions to go public are often referred to as unicorns.

| V Rally | After a large sell-off in the market, there's a tendency for the market to bounce back right away. It's caused by computerized trading programs. The term derives from how the move appears on a chart. Also known as the *Rubber Band Effect*. |

Summary:

This chapter explained the various slang terms used in the stock market to allow people to understand the language and culture of Wall Street. Terms like bear market, bull market, and blue chip. The chapter also provides examples of how slang can be used in conversations and also explains different stock market concepts, such as painting the tape, misery index, the quadruple witching hour, and Joe Granville Wednesday. It also explains the importance of knowing the language of the stock market, as it signals that you belong to the community.

Action Steps:

1. Learn the basics of investing slang.

2. Memorize a few key investing terms to use in conversation.

3. Become familiar with the different types of sides in the stock market, such as buy-side and sell-side.

4. Familiarize yourself with common stock market slang words, such as "bear market," "bull market," and "blue chip."

5. Understand the meaning of phrases like "gentlemen prefer bonds," "buy & hold," and "all the boats rise."

CHAPTER 12
Conclusion

S*tuck on the Stock Market* is designed to be part 2 of my book *Wealth Building for Beginners*. If you haven't read part 1, it might be a good idea to add it to your book list. There are three phases to building wealth from scratch. Phase one is simply understanding the general do's and don'ts on the road to achieving a basic surplus and protecting your income from loss. Phase two is the accumulation and surplus growth. Phase three is distribution and systematic ways to spend your money so it lasts a lifetime and there's enough to pass on to the next generation.

Stuck on the Stock Market is a guidebook for phase two. The stock market remains one of the best ways to accumulate significant money and build fortunes. Warren Buffett, Jim Simons, Ken Griffin, Ray Dalio, Carl Icahn, and John Paulson are among the world's top investors who have built wealth in the stock market. There are also many celebrities who are successful investors, such as Jessica Alba, Tyra Banks, Beyoncé, Jay-Z, Justin Bieber, George Clooney, Will Smith, and more. If you could have a conversation with any of these investors about achieving wealth from little means, what do you think they would tell you? Many of us will never speak to these individuals, but my guess is they would tell us to first spend less than we make and save, grow the savings outside of our emergency fund through diversified investments, and live as abundantly as possible without compromising the transfer of wealth to the next generation.

Let's look at some real examples of people who started with nothing and managed to build wealth in the stock market. Theodore Johnson was a common man who worked for the United Parcel Service (UPS) in 1924. He never made more than $14,000 a year, but every year he put 20% of his salary in company stock and eventually saw the value of his UPS stock grow to over $70 million.

My all-time favorite investor was the story of Oseola McCarty. She was a seamstress with just a sixth-grade education who was paid mostly in dollar bills and loose change her entire life. She never had a car or learned to drive, so she walked everywhere, including miles to the grocery store.

There are stories about thriftiness in which she cut the toes out of shoes that did not fit and bound her worn-out Bible with tape. Oseola saved her pennies in an interest-bearing account and eventually accumulated $280,000 by the time she retired at age 86. That was enough for her to set aside a pension to live on, donate to her church, leave small inheritances for three of her relatives, and donate the remainder of $150,000 to the University of Southern Mississippi, a school that had remained all-white until the 1960s. She wanted to help black students from southern Mississippi who wouldn't be able to go to the university because of financial hardship. Business leaders later matched her contribution, and many more people from around the country donated. She only invested in a savings account, but what if she would have known how to invest in the stock market?

This book discusses how to achieve a mix of diversified investments through the stock market. The first step is understanding investments and taking control of your money. Money is an object with no intrinsic value. It's neither good nor bad. How people spend money may be considered good or bad.

Growing up, I had no clue how to accumulate money outside of work and what the stock market was all about. If my household discussed the concepts in this book in my household at an early age, my wealth-building journey would've been fast-tracked. My goal with this book is to create household discussions in our communities about using the stock market to achieve economic wealth. The concepts are simplistic enough for us all to follow, ensuring that no one will ever be stuck with understanding the stock market. Keep this book on the kitchen table for frequent revisits. It's great with eggs and bacon.

The stock market has created an enormous amount of wealth over the years. Investing in stocks on average, the S&P 500, which includes 500 of the largest U.S. publicly traded companies, has returned 8% to 12% annually. However, be aware that the stock market doesn't go up every year. The S&P 500 typically falls three out of every 10 years. Some drops can feel quite brutal, and their level of volatility isn't for everyone. But if you can manage your fear, stocks have the potential to earn significantly higher returns than other investment options over the long term. Remember investing for lifetime goals. "Compounding interest is the eighth wonder of the world. He who understands it, earns it; he who doesn't pays it." – Albert Einstein. Investing in the stock market could offer you compounded returns. Getting in early and saving often is always better. Most bank savings accounts give you simple interest.

Many new investors are looking to make it big and fast when investing in the stock market. They often chase returns and search for the next big thing. It's important to note it's about making sure you have a good amount of time in the market not trying to time when you enter and exit the market. It's not a single night in a casino where you either go big or go home.

My favorite quote about the stock market was made by Warren Buffet. "If you don't find a way to make money while you sleep, you will work until you die." With inflation and taxes, simply saving cash will be a guaranteed loss on investment every year. Only by investing can you outpace inflation and taxation. The primary reason people invest in the stock market is the potential to earn higher returns. The stock market is designed to go up over time. If you don't invest, you're missing out on opportunities to increase your financial worth. With investing in the stock market, you can start investing with little money or skill, diversify your portfolio easily, and achieve long-term returns. The benefit of its liquidity can also help with achieving short-term goals. Let's build your financial investing journey.

We've all been taught that money cannot buy happiness. The truth is that recent studies have proven that money can make us happier. Research shows that the more you give to others, the happier you are. It's not the amount of money you spend, but how you decide to spend it that matters. "Everyday spending choices unleash a cascade of biological and emotional effects that are detectable right down to saliva," says Harvard's Elizabeth Dunn. Money is spiritual. Anyone who has become truly wealthy knows the truth. The only way to become wealthy, and stay wealthy, is to find a way to do more for others than anyone else is doing in an area that people really value. If you become a blessing in other people's lives, you too will be blessed.

Money is only one way to be a blessing, but it's a blessing. It's a form of freedom. I want to use this book as a vehicle to help you develop enough confidence in the stock market so that you can be a force for good through your economic gains.

Throughout my work, I've become obsessed with bringing the same comprehensive service, resources, and tools that wealthy families have become accustomed to, but my vision is to do it for people with far less money. Ignorance isn't bliss, as ignorance is a pain in the financial world. Information without execution is poverty. "Let's use the powerful machine of the stock market in an attempt to earn more so we can give more." — Edward R. Williams

Summary:

Stuck On The Stock Market is a guide to building wealth through the stock market, discussing the three phases of wealth building—understanding, accumulating, and distributing—with examples of people who have achieved wealth from nothing. It includes tips from the world's top investors, such as Warren Buffett, and encourages readers to save, diversify investments, and be generous with their money. Money can be a force for good and investing in the stock market can help with long-term returns

Action Steps:

1. Read my first book, *Wealth Building for Beginners*.

2. Create a plan to spend less than you make and save.

3. Understand the do's and don'ts of the stock market.

4. Invest in a diversified portfolio with a long-term view.

5. Make financial choices that will bring happiness.

"Congratulations! Because you are taking your first steps toward expanding your wealth by purchasing and reading my book, I will gift you a complimentary consultation with my team of licensed professionals and provide you with our Wealth Starter Kit. Go to https://edwardrwilliams.com/wealth-kit/ to receive my gift. Let's build your wealth!" – Edward.

Stock Market and Investing Education Worksheet

_____

_____

_____

_____

_____

_____

_____

_____

_____

_____

_____

_____

_____

_____

_____

_____

Set your daily habit goal for reading at least one source of information about the stock market.

What is your go-to source for daily learning about the stock market?

_____

_____

_____

_____

_____

_____

_____

Share this goal with someone and have them hold you accountable for achieving this goal.

Who will you choose?

_____

_____

_____

_____

_____

_____

_____

Define Your Current Financial Objectives Worksheet

Make a list of your current financial objectives and include today's date.

_____

_____

_____

_____

_____

_____

_____

_____

_____

_____

_____

_____

_____

_____

_____

_____

Of the objectives, you have added in question one, which objective is the most important and why?

_____

_____

_____

_____

_____

_____

List some obstacles that could get in the way of you achieving your most important objective.

_____

_____

_____

_____

_____

_____

List some ways you can overcome those obstacles that would stop you from achieving your most important current financial goal.

_____

_____

_____

_____

_____

_____

_____

Define Your One-Month Financial Objective Worksheet

Make a list of your one-month financial objectives and include today's date.

_____

_____

_____

_____

_____

_____

_____

_____

_____

_____

_____

_____

_____

_____

_____

Of the objectives, you have added in question one, which objective is the most important and why?

_____

_____

_____

_____

_____

_____

_____

List some obstacles that could get in the way of you achieving your most important objective.

_____

_____

_____

_____

_____

_____

_____

List some ways you can overcome those obstacles that would stop you from achieving your most important one-month financial goal.

_____

_____

_____

_____

_____

_____

_____

Define Your Six-Month Financial Objectives Worksheet

Make a list of your six-month financial objectives and include today's date.

_____

_____

_____

_____

_____

_____

_____

_____

_____

_____

_____

_____

_____

_____

_____

_____

Of the objectives, you have added in question one, which objective is the most important and why?

_____

_____

_____

_____

_____

_____

List some obstacles that could get in the way of you achieving your most important objective.

_____

_____

_____

_____

_____

_____

List some ways you can overcome those obstacles that would stop
you from achieving your most important six-month financial goal.

_____

_____

_____

_____

_____

_____

_____

Define Your One-Year Financial Objectives Worksheet

Make a list of your one-year financial objectives and include today's date.

_____

_____

_____

_____

_____

_____

_____

_____

_____

_____

_____

_____

_____

_____

_____

Of the objectives, you have added in question one, which objective is the most important and why?

_____

_____

_____

_____

_____

_____

List some obstacles that could get in the way of you achieving your most important objective.

_____

_____

_____

_____

_____

_____

List some ways you can overcome those obstacles that would stop you from achieving your most important one-year financial goal.

_____

_____

_____

_____

_____

_____

_____

Develop an Emergency Fund

_____

_____

_____

_____

_____

_____

_____

List all of your monthly expenses below.

_____

_____

_____

_____

_____

_____

_____

Now take that number and multiply it by 3 months or 6 months. If you are more conservative, have 6 months' savings in case of an emergency, so you do not have to sell any of your investments.

_____

_____

_____

_____

_____

_____

_____

If you do not have the 3 or 6 months of savings, you can then calculate how long it will take you to get there by subtracting your expenses from your monthly net income after taxes have been taken out. Calculate that below if you do not currently have an emergency fund.

_____

_____

_____

_____

_____

_____

Pay Down Your Debt

Add all your debt to the chart below:(Loans, Mortgages, College Debt, Credit Cards, Personal Loans, etc.)

Start with the highest Monthly Payments and work your way down.

Debt	Balance	Payment	Order

Now, choose the debt with the highest payment and the lowest balance and add a 1 in the order column. This is the debt you start paying extra on to reduce the balance to zero, to then not have a minimum payment for this debt. The savings from not paying this debt can be applied to the next highest payment with the lowest balance. Repeat until your last debt; likely, your mortgage is the remaining debt.

3 Month Vision Worksheet *How I'd like my life to be*

INSTRUCTIONS: Allow yourself 20 minutes of quiet time to consider these questions that help you create and shape your vision for your next 3 months. Write your answers in the PRESENT tense, and be as SPECIFIC as you can.

1. How do I want my life to be? Write below how you'd like each area to be in 3 months' time:

i) Personal Life, Home and Family

ii) Career, Work and Business Life

iii) Health and Well-being

iv) Finances and Wealth Building

v) Community, Friendships

vi) Spiritual and Learning

vii) Write anything else, that you perhaps haven't mentioned yet here:

2. What if there were no obstacles?

3. Who do you need to BE to achieve this? I need to be someone who is

4. If there was one important CHANGE you could make over the next 3 months, what would it be?

5. My THEME for the next 3 months is: _____

BACKGROUND

- We live busy lives and for many of us, finding time to ponder and reflect on what we want from life seems a waste of our precious time - or simply a distraction from the other 101 things we have on our lists.
- But if you're not clear on what you want it's impossible to have direction - we end up going wherever life takes us. We could end up anywhere or everywhere.
- Not knowing what we want also makes it hard to say "No" to others. How can we prioritise ourselves when we have nothing to work towards for ourselves? We have no REASON to say no.
- Having goals also gives us purpose in life. When we KNOW what we want, we can get focused and ask ourselves, "Does this move me towards my goals - or away from?"
- "If you don't know what you want, you'll end up with what you get!" So, let's get started.

INSTRUCTIONS

1) Create a space in your busy schedule.
2) Find a quiet spot - or a nice cosy coffee shop where you won't be interrupted by your normal life.
3) Answer the questions below!

Part 1 - Brainstorming Ideas

The purpose of this exercise is to brainstorm goal ideas and identify 5 ideas that could be turned into goals.

i. So, with each of the 2 lists below, aim for **as many items as you CAN** from big to small - ANYthing and EVERYthing you can think of.

ii. Then CIRCLE 5 of your ideas as possible goals - the first 5 things that grab you, get you inspired or excited.

1. List below all the **things** you want to **BE, DO and HAVE** in the next 1-5 years:

2. List below everything you **DON'T WANT** to **BE, DO and HAVE** in the next 1-5 years:

Part 2 - Refining your Ideas

Working towards unexciting goals is a hard slog. So we're just checking your 5 potential goals and making sure they're exciting for you before you go any further.

Write the Top 5 items you MAY like to work with: Pick 5 things you might like to work on for the coming year. You can use the 5 ideas from Part 1 or anything else you can think of that you may want to work on in the year ahead.	What would achieving this goal do for YOU? How will you FEEL, How will your life be different?	How EXCITING is this goal? Score it out of 10 below
1.		_____ / 10
2.		_____ / 10
3.		_____ / 10
4.		_____ / 10
5.		_____ / 10

Are you Excited? If your Excitement Score is 8 or more – Congratulations, you have found great goals!
But if your Excitement Score is less than 8, you may want to reflect on what would make that goal's score higher before continuing with it.

Part 3 - Set Your Wealth Goals!
Now it's time to pick 3 wealth goals to actually work with. The best wealth goals are:

a) **Aligned with your values.** The more a goal aligns with your inner or core values – the EASIER it will be to achieve. (NB. You can achieve goals that don't align with your values but it's usually harder and less satisfying.) Trust your gut instinct here.
b) **Stated in the positive.** Focus on what you WANT ie. "I want healthy fingernails" rather than "I want to stop biting my nails." This gives you a clear visual to work towards rather than a constant reminder of what you don't want.
c) **SPECIFIC!** The more specific you are, the easier it is to keep steering in the right direction - and the easier it is to achieve!

Write below the 3 Goals you WILL actually work with: Review what you've done so far and choose 3 goals for yourself. What would you be disappointed if you DIDN'T achieve?	Why bother? What outcome are you looking for? WHY do you want this goal? What are the BENEFITS to you?	WHEN will you achieve it by? A date to aim for & inspire you, not beat yourself up with	HOW will you know you've achieved your goal? What and how can you prove it has been completed?
1. _____ _____	• • •	Month Year _____ / 2____	
2. _____ _____	• • •	Month Year _____ / 2____	
3. _____ _____	• • •	Month Year _____ / 2____	

Excellent! Now let's take a look at how you can help yourself achieve these and how you might get in your own way.

Part 4 - Preparing for Success

i. Success Accelerators:
What can I start doing, stop doing, do more or less of that will help me achieve my goals?

_____

_____

_____

ii. Smash those Obstacles:
What could get in the way? If you were going to sabotage yourself how would you do it?

_____

_____

_____

iii. What is the best advice I could give myself to make sure I achieve these goals?

_____

_____

_____

Part 5 - Taking Action

So, what ONE thing will you do for EACH goal in the next month? (Yes, you can start now!)

Write out ONE action you will complete towards EACH goal in the NEXT MONTH. This is the FIRST STEP. Break the action down into a smaller step or action until you can commit 100%. If you want to do more than one action, great, but there must be a minimum of ONE.

GOAL 1 Action _____ by _____

GOAL 2 Action _____ by _____

GOAL 3 Action _____ by _____

And finally, what ONE action will I start tomorrow? _____

Part 6 - Support and Commitment

WHO will help & support me? Who are my CHEERLEADING TEAM?

Eg. Your personal trainer, coach, a friend, gym-partner, family, a work colleague. Get specific as to how they can support you.

1. Who _____ HOW Specifically? _____

2. Who _____ HOW Specifically? _____

3. Who _____ HOW Specifically? _____

Who will you have to BE to achieve these goals? _____

❑ **I am committed to achieving my goals**   **Signed** _____

Congratulations! Just one more step. To really COMMIT to your goals, complete the Goal Summary Sheet on the next page.

Part 7 - Take Off!

Want to commit one stage further to your wealth goals? Here is a summary sheet to help you:

Annual Goal-Setting
SUMMARY SHEET

YOUR COMPANY NAME/LOGO	My **CHEERLEADERS** are: *See part 6*
	1. _____
	2. _____
	3. _____

My **Wealth Goals** are: *See part 3 of this worksheet*

1. I _____ by _____

2. I _____ by _____

3. I _____ by _____

The **BENEFITS to me** of my GOALS are: *See part 3 of this worksheet (under why bother?)*	My **KEY Action Steps** are: *See part 5 of this worksheet*
1. _____	1. _____
2. _____	_____ by _____
3. _____	2. _____
My Success Accelerators: *See part 4 of this worksheet*	_____ by _____
1. _____	3. _____
2. _____	_____ by _____
3. _____	*Signed:* _____
	Date: _____

THOUGHT	For a free initial consultation by **Edward R. Williams, go to:**
"Even if you're on the right track, you'll get run over if you just sit there." **James Allen**	http://www.yourcompanyname.com

STAY ON TRACK

Now you have completed the Summary Sheet, cut it out and put it somewhere you will see it regularly like your fridge or bathroom mirror.

INSTRUCTIONS:
- Allow yourself 30 minutes of quiet time to consider these questions that help you create and shape a vision for your future.
- Work through the questions in the order below and write your answers in the PRESENT tense.

1. What is your ultimate wealth building goal? Do you want to retire early? Do you have a plan as to what your life would be like in retirement?

2. What if there were no obstacles?

3. What do you want to be doing (career and personal life):

i) 10 years from now

ii) 5 years from now

iii) 2 years from now

iv) 1 year from now

v) 6 months from now

vi) 3 months from now

Why we want our goals is totally unique to us. A pay-rise may mean self-esteem and validation, or it could mean security, a holiday or getting married. Once we understand WHY we want our goals, and why we want our goals NOW, it's easier to focus, go the "extra mile" and find that extra energy to put into our goals.

To get the most out of this exercise, I want you to be *totally honest* with yourself and lose the self-judgement. Write whatever pops into your head - however silly or boring it might seem.

Write Your Biggest Wealth Goal Here:

1. First, score out of 10, how motivated you are currently to achieve this goal: ____ / 10

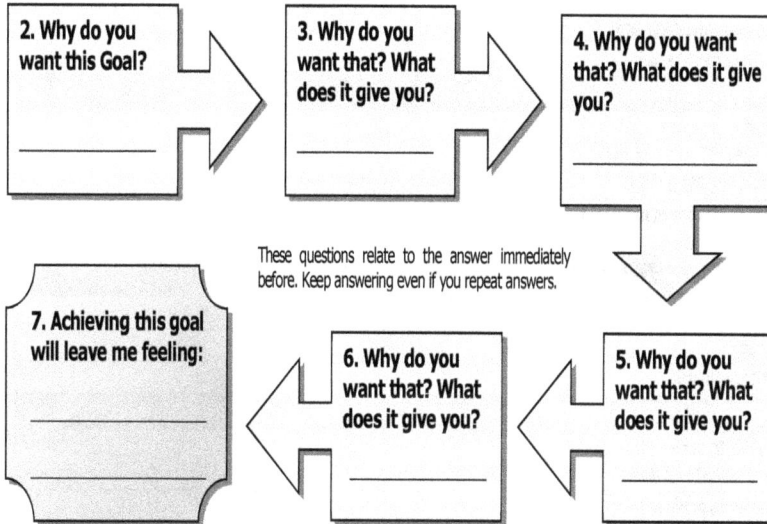

2. Why do you want this Goal?
_____

3. Why do you want that? What does it give you?
_____

4. Why do you want that? What does it give you?
_____

These questions relate to the answer immediately before. Keep answering even if you repeat answers.

7. Achieving this goal will leave me feeling:
_____
_____

6. Why do you want that? What does it give you?
_____

5. Why do you want that? What does it give you?
_____

Now you understand why you want your goal and how you want to feel. But to be really motivated, you need to be clear on one final question, **"Why do you want this goal now?"**

8. So, what circumstances in your life make this wealth goal important to you right now? Why not next year?
_____

What's your hidden treasure?

So, now that you understand your true motivations, how does this change the way you think about your goal?

9. I am now motivated to achieve this goal: ____ / 10 (If your motivation score is not 8 or above, why do you have this goal? Is it really your goal?)

10. What did you learn about yourself & your goal? What will you do differently? _____

Write Your SMART Wealth Goal Here _____

(Pick one goal to work with. Then see next page for description of SMART and help with writing successful goals)

_____ **by** ____ Day ____ Month ____ Year

Motivation	
WHY I want this goal (the 'outcome/s' you are looking for)	
List ALL the Benefits here (of achieving your goal)	
The BIG Benefit (of achieving goal)	
What is the PAIN? (of not achieving your goal)	
Achieving this Goal will also help me (other areas)	
Obstacles (also known as your secondary gain)	
I need to be aware that the BENEFIT to me of NOT completing my goals is	
Other obstacles to my success include	
Set Goal Levels (eg. your goal could vary on time, quantity, quality)	
MINIMUM	
TARGET	
EXTRAordinary	
How will you need to BE different? (a worthwhile goal often requires us to look at / do things differently)	
In order to achieve this goal I will START doing	
In order to achieve this goal I will STOP doing	
In order to achieve this goal I will need to BE someone who is	
Moving Forwards (eg. things, people, personal qualities, information, knowledge, skills, finance etc.)	
Resources available	
Resources I will need	
Taking ACTION (make these things EASILY achievable so you feel good about taking action!)	
3 steps I will complete in the next WEEK that move me closer to my goals	1. 2. 3.
3 steps I can complete in the next MONTH that move me closer to my goals	1. by 2. by 3. by

ALL ABOUT SMART WEALTH GOALS - They are:

1) Stated in the POSITIVE. We tend to get what we focus on. Whenever we say "I want to stop biting my fingernails" our brain has to first build a picture of what you DON'T want – bitten fingernails - in order not to do it. Try NOT thinking of an alligator biting your toe...

EXAMPLES

Eg. "I have healthy fingernails" rather than "I want to stop biting my nails"

Eg. "I weigh 150lbs" rather than "I want to lose 20lbs"

2) Stated in the PRESENT TENSE. This helps the brain to assume you will be successful!

EXAMPLES

Eg. On 30th September I have healthy fingernails/have a new job/am running a mile in 8 minutes

3) Use the Acronym "SMART"

- **S**pecific (the more specific you are the easier your goal is to achieve)
- **M**easurable (so you know when you have achieved it)
- **A**ction-oriented (ie. you can DO something about it! Is it within your control? ie. Winning the lottery is not a "SMART" goal)
- **R**ealistic (Goals need to be both challenging to inspire you AND realistic so you set yourself up for success)
- **T**ime-Bound (has a deadline)

For maximum success, **ENVISION YOUR WEALTH GOAL:** Describe a day in your life once this goal is completed. Imagine first waking up, describe how you feel. Now think about what you see and hear and physically feel. Fully describe your day now this goal is completed. Who are you? Where are you? What's important to you now?	

FINALLY that goals are there to INSPIRE you, not to beat yourself up with!

"Rocking Chair" Life Vision

INSTRUCTIONS:
- Do you ever wonder what your life dream is? This exercise helps you see the vision you *already have within you* for your life.
- Allow yourself 20 minutes of quiet time to ponder and write your answer in the space below!
- This is about YOU, so let your imagination go, **write a story and paint a picture of your life with words.**

Now, take a moment to REALLY imagine you are blissfully happy and healthy AND 90 years old. You're **sitting in your rocking chair** and looking back over your **IDEAL life**.

1. **Who are you** as a person? What is it about you that **people value**?

2. What have you **achieved?** What are you **proud of**? What added meaning to your life and gives you a sense of **fulfillment**?

3. Perhaps consider how your life unfolded in the following areas; **Family**, **Friends**, **Significant Other**, **Wealth**, **Career**, **Health** (emotional, spiritual and physical), your **Home**, what you did for **Fun and Leisure**, what you **Learned** about, what you did in **Service**, **Leadership** or in your **Community**.

4. Finally I wonder what you can **see** around you? What are you **feeling**? What can you **hear**? What SHOWS you're truly happy?

Tip: The complete picture may not magically arrive, just put pen to paper NOW and write – see what happens!

Retirement - or Big Birthday - Party Visioning Exercise

BACKGROUND:

- This visioning exercise involves you imagining some point in the future when you're going to retire. If you don't work (or can't imagine retiring) it could also be a "Big" Birthday party, perhaps your 60th, 65th or 70th Birthday.
- This party has been organized to celebrate you and a substantial change you're making in your life. Are you retiring - or maybe you're moving somewhere new? Perhaps you're going travelling or embarking on a new creative career? Only you know!
- However you got here, a big party is being held in your honour. This party is celebrating YOU.

So, take a moment to imagine that you're at a party all about you! Someone has written a speech celebrating you. What would it say? Use the question prompts below to help you write the speech that someone will read ABOUT you in the space below.

1. How old are you? Who is at the party? Where is the party being held?
2. What have you achieved in your family, career, wealth, business, community or in the world?
3. What is it about you that the **people at the party truly value**?
4. What would YOU want to be said about you? What would you be disappointed if it was not said?
5. What did you do that was truly amazing? Where did you surprise yourself? Where did you surprise others? What are you MOST proud of? What mistakes did you make, that you can laugh about now?
6. What is the essence of you that you would want to be captured in that retirement or birthday speech?
7. **Optional:** Where are you going next in your life? What are you excited to spend more time doing? How do your friends and family fit into your life going forwards?

Final Tip: Don't worry about writing a "good speech" - instead concentrate on what the speaker might say - if it helps, imagine this is a first draft of the speech, just to capture the key points. And remember to write the speech in the 3rd person eg. "Sarah/Auntie Sarah has always...":

"Life is a Celebration!" Edward R. Williams

"Newspaper Article" Writing Exercise

BACKGROUND:
- This visioning exercise involves you imagining you have achieved a great milestone in your life or career.
- What would success look like for you?
- It could be an award you've received, a book you've written, something you've established or created. It could be a fund-raising goal you reached, a feat of travel, charitable activities or something else.
- Now, write an article as if written by a newspaper about the recent milestone and successes you have achieved.

Tips

1. Write from 250-500 words in in the PAST tense.

2. Mention yourself, anyone who helped you and any sources quoted - by name.

3. Remember to give a little background including recent successes and other relevant highlights.

4. What does your success MEAN for the people reading it - how do the readers benefit?

5. OPTIONAL: What newspaper would you like to be featured in? Try (as best you can) to write in that newspaper's style.

Final Tip: Don't worry about grammar or spelling here - this is about capturing your vision and essence.

Whether we achieve our goals depends on whether we take action. But what decides whether we take action in the first place? How motivated you are! So, simply **pick your Top 3 wealth goals**, then **answer the questions below**. Keep writing even if you repeat your answers. The information below will help you feel clear, focused and more motivated to achieve your goals.

Write Wealth Goal No. 1 Here:	Write Wealth Goal No. 2 Here:	Write Wealth Goal No. 3 Here:
Why do you want this Goal? What does it give you?	Why do you want this Goal? What does it give you?	Why do you want this Goal? What does it give you?
And why do you want that? What does that give you?	And why do you want that? What does that give you?	And why do you want that? What does that give you?
And why do you want that? What does that give you?	And why do you want that? What does that give you?	And why do you want that? What does that give you?
And why do you want that? What does that give you?	And why do you want that? What does that give you?	And why do you want that? What does that give you?
What will this goal help you feel?	What will this goal help you feel?	What will this goal help you feel?

INSTRUCTIONS: Everyone says how important it is to have goals, but sometimes we don't know where to start. The purpose of this exercise is to **brainstorm** potential goals and **identify up 10 possible areas that could be turned into goals.** You can do all 5 stages in one sitting, but it works well to allow yourself 1-2 weeks to complete all the steps - including returning to your initial brainstorm to add anything you may think of afterwards!

1. **FIRST, BRAINSTORM a Wacky, Wild List of everything you want in your lifetime!**
   - List below all the **Wacky, Wild** (and normal!) **things** you want to **BE, DO and HAVE** in life!
   - Aim for **at least 50 items** from big to small, ANYthing and EVERYthing you can think of.
   - **Write as quickly as you can,** keeping your **answers brief** and **on one page.** This is a brainstorming exercise, so nothing is ruled out. **Everything should be included** from the mundane to the extreme.
   - As this is a 'stream of consciousness' approach, **duplicates, silly and meaningless answers are just fine.**

2. **DISCOVER WHICH GOALS are most meaningful for you:** Now, beside each item on your Wacky Wild Wealth Goal Brainstorm List on page 1, give it a score of 1 for EACH element on the 'Wheel of Life' that would be improved should you achieve that goal. The maximum possible score for any item on your brainstorming list is therefore 8.

EXAMPLE:

If you had "Own a Ferrari" as one of your goals, would it improve your 1) Career? 2) Money? 3) Health? 4) Friends and Family? 5) Significant Other/Partner? etc. Perhaps it would **score a total of 1** on your wheel (Fun).

And if you had "Get a Dog" as a goal, would it improve your 1) Career? 2) Money? 3) Health? 4) Friends and Family? 5) Significant Other/Partner? etc. Perhaps this goal would **score a total of 4** on your wheel (Health, Personal Growth, Fun, Home).

The elements/headings from the Wheel of Life are:

1. Career
2. Money/Wealth
3. Health
4. Friends and Family
5. Significant Other/Partner
6. Personal Growth and Learning
7. Fun, Leisure and Recreation
8. Physical Environment/Home

Note: Be honest – only give it a point if it TRULY improves an element on your wheel. And yes, you can score ½ points!

3. **REVIEW YOUR LEARNINGS.** Take another look at your Wacky Wild Wealth Goal Brainstorm List on page 1:

Which goals have the highest scores? _____

_____

Which goals have the lowest scores? _____

_____

What surprises (if any) are there as you review your scores? _____

_____

_____

Where do you normally place your focus in life? Why do you think that is? _____

_____

_____

What have you learned about yourself so far from this exercise? What common themes are there? What else?_____

_____

_____

4. **SELECT 10 items from your list as possible goals.** These don't have to be your highest scoring items, but they probably will have high scores. And now in one brief sentence write below WHY the goal is important to you.

   IMPORTANT NOTE: If you are unable to come up with a good justification – ask yourself why is it still on the list?

   1. _____ is important to me because_____

      _____

   2. _____ is important to me because_____

      _____

   3. _____ is important to me because_____

      _____

   4. _____ is important to me because_____

      _____

   5. _____ is important to me because_____

      _____

   6. _____ is important to me because_____

      _____

   7. _____ is important to me because_____

      _____

   8. _____ is important to me because_____

      _____

   9. _____ is important to me because_____

      _____

   10. _____ is important to me because_____

So, you now have 10 possible goals to work with. Finally, just before we wrap up this exercise, ponder:

5. **What are the key learnings that you'd like to make a note of and take away?**

1st Key Observation/Learning   _____

2nd Key Observation/Learning   _____

3rd Key Observation/Learning   _____

Your Weekly Wealth Scorecard

Date: _____

ACTION	MON	TUES	WED	THURS	FRI	SAT	SUN	TARGET	SCORE	HIT?

What action needs improvement this week?

Phone: 888-7-Retire   www.edwardrwilliams.com